THE ESSENTIAL

TRANSCENDENTALISTS

THE ESSENTIAL
TRANSCENDENTALISTS

Edited and Introduced by

RICHARD G. GELDARD

JEREMY P. TARCHER / PENGUIN
a member of Penguin Group (USA) Inc.
New York

For Alec and Jim

JEREMY P. TARCHER/PENGUIN
Published by the Penguin Group
Penguin Group (USA) Inc., 375 Hudson Street, New York, New York 10014, USA •
Penguin Group (Canada), 90 Eglinton Avenue East, Suite 700, Toronto, Ontario M4P 2Y3,
Canada (a division of Pearson Penguin Canada Inc.) • Penguin Books Ltd, 80 Strand,
London WC2R 0RL, England • Penguin Ireland, 25 St Stephen's Green, Dublin 2,
Ireland (a division of Penguin Books Ltd) • Penguin Group (Australia), 250 Camberwell
Road, Camberwell, Victoria 3124, Australia (a division of Pearson Australia Group Pty Ltd) •
Penguin Books India Pvt Ltd, 11 Community Centre, Panchsheel Park, New Delhi–110 017,
India • Penguin Group (NZ), Cnr Airborne and Rosedale Roads, Albany,
Auckland 1310, New Zealand (a division of Pearson New Zealand Ltd) • Penguin Books
(South Africa) (Pty) Ltd, 24 Sturdee Avenue, Rosebank, Johannesburg 2196, South Africa

Penguin Books Ltd, Registered Offices: 80 Strand, London WC2R 0RL, England

Library of Congress Cataloging-in-Publication Data

The essential transcendentalists / edited and introduced by Richard G. Geldard.
p.   cm.
Includes bibliographical references.
ISBN 1-58542-434-X
1. Transcendentalism (New England).   2. Transcendentalists (New England).
I. Geldard, Richard G.
B905.E87   2005   2005044016
141'.3'0973—dc22

Printed in the United States of America
3   5   7   9   10   8   6   4   2

Quotations from Wallace Stevens, *The Collected Poems*, Alfred A. Knopf, Inc., 1954,
appear by permission of Random House, Inc.

CONTENTS

I. PRIMARY TEXTS

II. INDIVIDUAL VOICES

III. THE TRANSCENDENTAL HERITAGE

I

PRIMARY TEXTS

INTRODUCTION TO THE
PRIMARY TEXTS

The first questions are still to be asked. Let any man bestow a thought on himself, how he came hither, and whither he tends, and he will find that all the literature, all the philosophy that is on record, have done little to dull the edge of inquiry. The globe that swims so silently with us through the sea of space, has never a port, but with its little convoy of friendly orbs pursues its voyage through the signs of heaven, to renew its navigation again forever. The wonderful tidings our glasses and calendars give us concerning the hospitable lights that hang around us in the deep, do not appease but inflame our curiosity; and in like manner, our culture does not lead to any goal, but its richest results of thought and action are only new preparation.

—RALPH WALDO EMERSON, "The Senses and the Soul"

Those who seek to uncover the mysteries of the truth of reality may not appear to be a rare, lonely breed, but those who devote their lives to the single-minded pursuit of such mysteries certainly are. They do their deepest searching alone, usually from a stance outside the confines of systems and institutions, because those who work inside these frameworks are, with few exceptions, seldom able to divest themselves of the demands of their confinement. It is a characteristic of genius to remain aloof, autonomy being primary in the search for the truth of reality.

Looking back today at all the figures associated with New England Transcendentalism, we see Ralph Waldo Emerson and Henry David Thoreau as the dominant figures. Along with their close friends Amos Bronson Alcott and Margaret Fuller, who also maintained a strict autonomy, these individuals chose independence as their path in life and had to find their way without formal structures to support them. What is also striking about their journeys is their conviction that the truth of reality was based on some principle other than materialism and that the task of uncovering that principle and describing it to the world would be their task in life.

For Emerson and the rest of the Transcendentalists, the universe was sustained by something deeper, more fundamental, than the material laws of chemical, biological and physical reaction. They called that something deeper *idealism*. To them, the religious answer, that the operative principle was called *God*, was an evasion, a setting aside of the question of reality. It was an abdication of reason, that gift of the Enlightenment, which fed both materialist and idealist in different ways. The materialist world of sense was only superficial, an illusion, whereas the truth of reality was based on something much more profound. Emerson put it this way in his essay "The Transcendentalist":

These two modes of thinking are both natural, but the idealist contends that his way of thinking is in higher nature. He concedes all that the other affirms, admits the impressions of sense, admits their coherency, their use and beauty, and then asks the materialist for his grounds of assurance that things are as his senses represent them. But I, he says, affirm facts not affected by the illusions of sense, facts which are of the same nature as the faculty which reports them, and not liable to doubt.

Access to what Emerson called "higher nature" was achieved by passing through the gate guarded by self-reflective thought, what in his essay "The American Scholar" he would call "Man Thinking." It is the examined life spoken of by Socrates and then by generations of those who seek after the ground of being. And at the core of this quest was the conviction that the individual mind was a fragment of the universal mind and that an overarching consciousness was the common element in which we all take our life. That conviction, more than any other, drew the solitary voices of Transcendentalism into a unified vision.

Each generation, each age, has its forms of expression, its way of confronting the mysteries of existence and being. Even though what we have come to term New England Transcendentalism was but a brief flowering of this idealism, it has demonstrated a remarkable staying power, mostly through the works of Emerson and Thoreau, works that have never been out of print since the movement ended in the 1850s. When we ask why New England Transcendentalism has experienced such staying power, we have to examine the broad spiritual themes underlying its more localized expression and rhetoric. Not only did the movement reflect German Romantic Idealism and the more ancient Perennial Philosophy, but it also embodied more contemporary ideas of universal consciousness and spiritual idealism. These are concepts very prominent in our own time.

Therefore, the material chosen for inclusion in this book is intended to reflect these broader, deeper, less superficial concerns. When we seek answers to fundamental questions about who we are and how we are to live, we find the contemporary landscape often littered with glib answers by the purveyors of programmatic advice of all kinds. Not so the Transcendentalists, who spoke to the practical problems of daily life while resisting the temptation to offer formulas or programs. Instead, they urged self-reliance and inner inquiry, and what is most helpful in their writings is the example they provide from their experience and the process they reveal as they went on their solitary journeys to discover for themselves the truth of reality. The word *essential* in the title of this book not only speaks to the choices made from the huge body of material available but also reflects a vision of what is essential in measuring the value and meaning of human life as seen through the lives and minds of what has come to be known as the Concord circle.

ESOTERIC INFLUENCES

As the decade of the 1820s dawned in and around Boston, Massachusetts, a few individuals associated with Harvard and with Unitarian Christianity began to feel the need to react to dogmas they perceived as stale and lifeless in order to restore a semblance of unity and harmony to the intellectual and spiritual life of their communities. In the case of Boston at that time, an added threat was the explosion of commercialism and associated materialism affecting daily life and ordinary thought, producing what Emerson would later call America's tendency toward "superficialness."

It was the ambition of the Transcendentalists in New England to create a coherent and unified vision that would eventually include elements of early Christianity, Greek philosophy, natural science, and artistic imagination. They wished to harmonize the growing estrangement among the fields of science, religion, and literature, to heal those widening schisms, and to bring about a revision of human nature consistent with a spiritually coherent philosophy.

In its full flowering, Transcendentalism was not just an isolated literary movement, nor was it merely theological revisionism. Rather, for the disparate and solitary individuals associated with it, Transcendentalism became the attempt to reconcile the disharmony in the fragmented world they experienced. Initially, they discovered a source for their vision of unity among pre-Christian esoteric traditions, closely connected with the Perennial Philosophy, that ancient wisdom tradition having its genesis in the Far East and, like a thin thread of thought, weaving its way west into the fabric of Greek, Roman, medieval, and Renaissance thought. Eventually, through English Romanticism, it made its way into the coarser materials making up the new world.

Originally, the Perennial Philosophy took its name from the work of Gottfried Leibniz (1646–1716), and it became a serious movement in England through Christian reformers like the Cambridge Platonists (John Smith and Ralph Cudworth) and Jacob Boehme in the seventeenth century. They were succeeded by William Blake and his followers, among them the Greek scholar Thomas Taylor, whose translations of Greek philosophy were influential in Emerson's circle. In our own time, the Perennial Philosophy made its presence known through Aldous Huxley and his 1946 anthology of the same name. Huxley defined this tradition as "the metaphysic that recognizes a divine Reality substantial to the world of things and lives and minds; the psychology that finds in the soul something similar to, or even identical with, divine Reality."[1]

In the 1830s those who were eventually called Transcendentalists generally subscribed to this central feature of Perennial thinking.

In that special sense, their movement was inevitably a religious one, and the cries of heresy at the time arose from men of the Church who saw in Transcendentalism a direct threat to traditional authority and biblical teachings. They were, of course, perfectly correct. The threat was very real. At stake was the authority of the Bible itself in establishing the nature of revelation and in holding up the separation between what was deemed human and what divine. As we shall see in the next section, "Individual Voices," Emerson's notion of "the infinitude of the private man" broke down that division and, at least for religion, drew a proverbial line in the sand.

To give a sense of what these heretics were studying at the time, here is what Emerson read in the general introduction to Thomas Taylor's translation of the complete works of Plato, about the nature of the philosophic quest:

Hence Socrates, in the Republic, speaking of the power of dialectic [true philosophic inquiry], says that it surrounds all disciplines like a defensive enclosure, and elevates those that use it, to the good itself, and the first unities; that it purifies the eye of the soul; establishes itself in true beings, and the one principle of all things, and ends at last in that which is no longer hypothetical. The power of dialectic, therefore, being thus great, and the end of this path so mighty, it must by no means be confounded with arguments which are alone conversant with opinion: for the former is the guardian of sciences, and the passage to it is through these, but the latter is perfectly destitute of disiplinative [*sic*] sciences. To which we may add, that the method of reasoning, which is founded in opinion, regards only that which is apparent; but the dialectic method endeavors to arrive at the one itself, always employing for this purpose the steps of ascent, and at last beautifully ends in the nature of the good.[2]

Here is an affirmation, inherent in the Perennial Philosophy, that it is possible for human beings to have direct communion with the One, or God, or Absolute, through the powers of the dialectic, which for Plato referred to that power of the soul that reasons scientifically through inquiry. Human beings, Plato said, live customarily in a false world of opinion, always equated with duality. The suggestion that the fundamental unities are to be found in dialectical inquiry became a touchstone for the Transcendentalists, even as their individual writings displayed great diversity of style and subject matter.

The influence of the Perennial Philosophy was, however, not an overt one among the Emerson circle. It was too far removed from current thinking and too mystical to suit the young and restless minds of Unitarian Boston. A more immediate challenge was to confront the prevailing philosophy of the times, represented by the empirical thinkers of the previous century, in a way that matched, at least in part, that empirical style. Also in matters of style was the so-called "common touch" introduced by the poetry of William Wordsworth (1770–1850). Here was language to be emulated among the good, plain-speaking people of America.

THE SCRAPED TABLE

Among the opposing forces influencing the development of Transcendentalism, hence major obstacles to be overcome on the path to unity, were the philosophies of John Locke (1632–1704) and David Hume (1711–1776), the two empirical thinkers most influential on the eighteenth century. Locke's notion of the *tabula rasa,* literally the "scraped table"—or the "blank slate," as it came to be called—was his description of the condition of the newborn human mind. His was a central image of post-Enlightenment rational thinking about the nature of the human instrument. Landing heavily on the side of nurture in the nature/nurture debate, Locke insisted on the overwhelming influence of experience in the shaping of consciousness. The mind, he argued, was an empty vessel ready to be filled, trained, and influenced for good or evil by experience alone. Locke's view became the dominant one among the materialists of the time.

The effect of this view was sufficiently reductive to attract vehement objectors, among them Immanuel Kant (1724–1804). Fortunately for our understanding of the human instrument, Kant was a genius in possession of a more penetrating mind than Locke's, and so was able to show, through intuitive argument and reasoned analysis, that Locke's understanding lacked the depth to describe reality. Subsequently, it was through Samuel Taylor Coleridge (1772–1834), father of the English Romantic movement, that the complexities of Kantian analysis spoke more clearly to thinkers in England and America.

But Locke was not the only rationalist to be answered. David Hume's skepticism, as well, was a substantial challenge, at least in regard to the nature and functioning of the human mind. Although he admitted to being unsatisfied with his own views of what exactly constituted the self, Hume nonetheless argued that when he looked into his mind, he could find nothing that was purely himself, as opposed to a perception of something external to it. He saw the human mind as a mere bundle of perceptions, constantly shifting with experience, with no core identity. In fact, Hume's extreme skepticism doubted even the existence of mind itself. This argument resulted in an attack on the individual's ability to trust in powers of personal insight. And it also challenged the very existence of consciousness, or essence, as a reality.

Emerson's wide-ranging speculative curiosity engaged the problem of how to answer Hume. As Robert D. Richardson told us in *Emerson: The Mind on Fire*,[3] one early instrument useful in that effort was the Scotsman Dugald Stewart's *Progress of Metaphysical, Ethical, and Moral Philosophy*, which was published in 1821 and which Emerson was reading as early as 1822.

In Stewart's words, "the doctrine of Mr. Hume . . . is an absolute and universal system of skepticism, professing to be derived from the very structure of the understanding, which . . . would render it impossible . . . to form an opinion upon any subject."[4] Hume's reductive arguments meant that the human mind was incapable of assigning any meaning to events or thoughts arising from mental experience, effectively rendering the human being helpless in making any sense of the world.

Hume's arguments questioned the notion that human beings possessed higher faculties of mind, including reason, intuition, and creative imagination with which to apprehend intimations of being and existence, and that as a result, spiritual insights were also excluded from individual perception. All of Emerson's instincts, as well as some of his direct experiences, rebelled against Hume's skepticism, and he was determined to find the proper means of formulating a worldview opposing it. It was not enough, however, simply to assert that Hume was wrong. What was needed was the use of all the human faculties, namely, intelligence, imagination, creativity, and the powers of observation.

EUROPEAN INFLUENCES

As most of the participants and subsequent commentators have affirmed, the major supporting arguments for the Transcendentalists came from Europe with the writings of Goethe, Wordsworth, Coleridge, and Thomas Carlyle. This quartet shared a common rejection of dogma and sects in religion and, most important, an aversion to reductive, material definitions of reality. They thought broadly, wrote expansively as well as daringly, and weathered the criticism of their tradition-bound cultures. Most important, they argued well, convincingly.

In Johann Wolfgang von Goethe (1749–1832), German, and then world, culture was presented with the epitome of the true generalist: poet, artist, scientist, and philosopher (of an unsystematic variety) as well as a man of the world. In *Representative Men,* Emerson held up Goethe as the example of the ideal writer: "What distinguishes Goethe for French and English readers is a property which he shares with his nation,—a habitual reference to interior truth."

For the Transcendentalists, Goethe was the best example, although an imperfect one they believed, of the seeker for the unity they upheld as the central goal of their quest. He was imperfect, in their estimate, because of his cavalier attitude toward social mores, particularly his flaunting of relationships outside of marriage. Despite these perceived character flaws, however, or even because of them, he emerged as a heroic figure. Against all the trends of the time, Goethe rejected dogmatic religious beliefs, sectarian differences, and the reductive specializations in science and literature. Only Shakespeare and Plato were given more honored places in Emerson's pantheon. Emerson said this of his hero's grasp of the multiplicity of existence:

> Goethe was the philosopher of this multiplicity; hundred-handed, Argus-eyed, able and happy to cope with this rolling miscellany of facts and sciences, and by his own versatility to dispose of them with ease; a manly mind, unembarrassed by the variety of coats of convention with which life had got encrusted, easily able by his subtlety to pierce these and to draw his strength from nature, with which he lived in full communion. What is strange too, he lived in a small town, in a petty state, in a defeated state, and in a time when Germany played no such leading part in the world's affairs as to swell the bosom of her sons with any metropolitan pride, such as might have cheered a French, or English, or once, a Roman or Attic genius. Yet there is no trace of provincial limitation in his muse. He is not a debtor to his position, but was born with a free and controlling genius.

Next in line stood William Wordsworth. Although he would later fade in importance amid the subsequent glories of Romantic poetry, Wordsworth was an early luminary in the Transcendental heavens. His "Intimations of Immortality" from *Recollections of Early Childhood* set a standard that poets, including Emerson, sought to emulate. Wordsworth's example was important for its natural style, autobiographical honesty, and depth of feeling. Amid the academic formalisms of the period, how these lines must have stirred the feelings, longings, and imaginations of these young seekers:

VIII
Thou, whose exterior semblance doth belie
Thy Soul's immensity;

Thou best Philosopher, who yet dost keep
Thy heritage, thou Eye among the blind,
That, deaf and silent, read'st the eternal deep,
Haunted for ever by the eternal mind,—
Mighty Prophet! Seer blest!
On whom those truths do rest,
Which we are toiling all our lives to find,
In darkness lost, the darkness of the grave;
Thou, over whom thy Immortality
Broods like the Day, a Master o'er a Slave,
A Presence which is not to be put by;
Thou little Child, yet glorious in the might
Of heaven-born freedom on thy being's height,
Why with such earnest pains dost thou provoke
The years to bring the inevitable yoke,
Thus blindly with thy blessedness at strife?
Full soon thy Soul shall have her earthly freight,
And custom lie upon thee with a weight
Heavy as frost, and deep almost as life!

Wordsworth's own commentary on this poem reflects the vision forming in the minds of his admirers in America. He said, "I was often unable to think of external things as having external existence, and I communed with all that I saw as something not apart from, but inherent in, my own immaterial nature."[5] This view of the immaterial nature of reality was consistent with the Eastern influences of the Perennial Philosophy, which saw the matter of the universe as illusory, the *maya* sustained by pure consciousness.

Thomas Carlyle (1795–1881), like Emerson, had trained for the clergy but rejected the ministry as too confining and overly dogmatic. The two met and became close friends during Emerson's first trip abroad in 1833. Carlyle was everything Emerson was not: outwardly warm, flamboyant, openly humorous, and more than happy to satirize anything pompous, false, or unjust. As Richardson points out, Emerson had read anonymous essays by Carlyle starting in 1826, but it was only weeks before he set sail for Europe that he learned the identity of the much admired writer. So it was a major goal of his journey to find Carlyle and engage him in serious conversation.[6]

Among those Emerson met on his trip to Europe, including Coleridge and Wordsworth, it was only Carlyle who proved a worthy companion and friend for life. What attracted Emerson to Carlyle was his intellectual grasp of the work of the German Idealists, including Goethe, and also his passionate response to the social ills of industrial England at the beginning of the nineteenth century. Always the reformer, Carlyle pressed the aristocracy and the newly enriched business class to meet their moral responsibilities, to provide clean, safe factories and decent wages. But always at the core of Carlyle's call for reform was an emphasis on the moral foundations of human life, the recognition that all human beings shared the same nature and mutual responsibility for one another.

The essential spiritual difference between the two was that for Carlyle, spirit meant moral conscience more than divine insight, and he criticized Coleridge for asserting that reason could apprehend spiritual truths. Carlyle's spiritual concerns were focused on human behavior rather than human perception. Despite these differences, though, the bond between Carlyle and Emerson was a strong one and would benefit both their writing careers as Transcendentalism came to the fore in America.

One of Emerson's final stops in England in 1833 was to call on the aging Coleridge. Although the interview was disappointing to the young Emerson, his appreciation for the early work of the father of the Romantic movement went unchecked. Years later, a copy of the James Marsh edition of Coleridge's *Aids to Reflection* was frequently close at hand on his table.

With Kant and Goethe as inspiration, Coleridge responded to the empiricists by carefully redefining the faculties of reason and understanding in the human mind. The reasoning faculty, he argued, was capable of a higher reception of divine things, which would then descend into the more cursive understanding for formulation and articulation. The Transcendentalists, Emerson in particular, would make the same argument as the basis for personal revelation and intuitive spiritual gnosis. In addition, they would argue, the mind has the capacity to discriminate between superficial impressions and deeper, intuitive hints from the whisperings of Universal Mind.

NEW ENGLAND INFLUENCES

Sampson Reed (1800–1880) was ahead of Emerson at Harvard and had prepared for the ministry at Divinity College. He withdrew from his studies there, however, because he encountered the work of Emanuel Swedenborg (1688–1772), mystic, scientist, and visionary. Giving up his preparation for the Unitarian ministry, Reed became a successful pharmacist and devoted his life and much of his subsequent wealth to the support of Swedenborg's New Church.

In 1826, Reed published the hundred-page *Observations on the Growth of the Mind*. It was an answer to Locke and a refinement of the mystical teachings of Swedenborg. In his journal for September of that year, Emerson noted his admiration for Reed's effort—was even moved to call it "revelation," so much did it demonstrate to him both originality and truth. The impression on Emerson and the other budding Transcendentalists would be substantial. Indeed, Emerson would incorporate many of the insights in Reed's *Observations* into his own *Nature* ten years later, and long afterward would list Reed as "one of his men."

The same could not be said, however, of Reed's appreciation for Emerson. In later years, Reed would have nothing good to say in behalf of the Transcendental movement. When the two disagreed over the philosophy of Swedenborg, for example, Reed told Emerson, "It is not so in your experience, but it is so in the other world." Rejecting the presentiment of duality, Emerson responded, "Other world? There is no other world; here or nowhere is the whole fact." The incident is a vivid example of the world of duality (Reed's) meeting a vision of greater unity (Emerson's).

This disagreement over the perception of reality exposed the fundamental difference between the orthodox and Transcendental views of reality. Although Emerson admired Swedenborg and chose him in *Representative Men* as the archetypal mystic in the historical search for the truth of reality, there was always this question of the nature of the world. In Emerson's case, as it would be in Thoreau's, the idea that "here or nowhere is the whole fact" meant that our task was to understand that the world of our sensory experience was an illusion and that its reality lay hidden from us but still within the world of nature. Somehow, they thought, if we penetrated to the true nature and laws of the world we experienced, all would eventually be revealed, including the nature of God. Connected to this view was a perception that consciousness was the mediating element.

Despite Reed's difference of opinion with Emerson, it was still his brilliant analysis of mind in *Observations* that provided the fresh vocabulary the Transcendentalists were seeking in order to articulate their views. As the examples in "Primary Sources" will show, Coleridge tended to sermonize with a syntax close to the King James Bible. Alcott, although very influential prior to Emerson's entrance onto the scene in 1836, was much too abstract, too prone to loftiness. Both Marsh and Reed, on the other hand, were closer to the desired tone and treatment of spiritual subject matter. Theirs would be the early influence most deeply felt and liberally applied.

James Marsh (1794–1842), like Reed, was not a Transcendentalist; rather he was an orthodox Protestant divine bent on revitalizing the troubled Church of his day. What he had in common with the thinking he helped influence, however, was the impulse to unify the fragmented worlds of religion and science dividing his culture. In fact, it was he—in 1829, just three years after Reed's *Observations*—who had the inspiration and dedication to publish an American edition of *Aids to Reflection,* and it was Marsh's preface to this book around which the group of dedicated scholars in Boston and Concord gathered to begin their spiritual revolution.

For example, one of this number, James Freeman Clarke (1810–1888), made a note in his autobiography, explaining the importance of the Marsh influence.

It was about the time of our senior year that Professor Marsh of Vermont University was reprinting Coleridge's "Friend" and his "Aids to Reflection" and his "Biographia Literaria." . . . Coleridge the philosopher confirmed my longing for a higher philosophy than that of John Locke. . . . Something within me revolted at all . . . attempts to explain soul out of sense, deducing mind from matter, or tracing the origin of ideas to nerves, vibrations, and vibratiuncles. So I concluded I had no taste for metaphysics and gave it up, until Coleridge showed me from Kant that though knowledge begins with experience it does not come from experience. Then I discovered that I was born a Transcendentalist.[7]

Foremost in this passage is Clarke's "longing" for a theory of the human instrument that was more expansive than what was being offered by the reductionism of John Locke. Second, he had an intuition from his own inner life that what he called "soul" had a life independent of his senses and nervous system. And third, until he discovered Coleridge, he had no use for metaphysics, which he assumed had become irrelevant under the influence of Locke and Hume. But now, in the light of Coleridge, there emerged a way to connect philosophy, theology, and epistemology to begin a search for a more harmonious vision of human nature. He was, as it were, reborn. His instinctive longing for the metaphysical quest for the ground of being was renewed.

This expression of intense feeling from Clarke adds the final element to the search for a viable philosophy among these early Transcendentalists. Without knowing it, they were searching for a way of seeing that incorporated both reason and feeling into a single vision. In other words, in order to experience unity, both heart and mind had to fuse into harmony. Feeling one thing and thinking another would only lead to suffering and doubt. The aim was to experience a harmony based on the most rigorous examination of both the world and the human instrument, seen as one.

Although the passion and intensity so characteristic of Transcendentalism in its beginnings had a rational foundation in Immanuel Kant's revision of Locke and Hume, Kant's formal arguments were impenetrable to all but the most dedicated and professionally trained philosophers. One particular sentence of his, however, was known and understood clearly: "I call all knowledge transcendental which is concerned, not with objects, but with our mode of knowing objects so far as this is possible *a priori*." This "mode of knowing" would be the key to a harmonious vision.

It was Coleridge who carried forward Kant's arguments with a more affirmative notion of what was possible to know by making a clear distinction between reason and understanding. Marsh, following along, interceded further by spelling out these distinctions in his preface to *Aids to Reflection*. It was, then, a gradual movement from Kant to Marsh, a stepping-down of the initial power generated from Kant's abstract arguments, that provided the language and the understanding for an average scholar seeking the truth of things.

As the selected excerpt from the preface to *Aids to Reflection* (see page 34), illustrates, Marsh's contribution was to give new credibility to powers of the individual mind. He accomplished this feat in the face of reductive arguments by affirming the mind's capacity to intuit the nature of things according to natural laws, which were simultaneously divine in character and confluent with nature in their execution. Like all similar thought associated with the Perennial Philosophy, Marsh wrote in his preface that the mind had access to the ground of being, or Absolute, and that this access did not depend on any intermediary structures or persons, although, he would also assert, ecclesiastical authority was a necessary check on rash claims of revelation. In effect, Marsh was too conservative to take the great leap into the Transcendental abyss.

Unlike Reed and Marsh, **Frederic Henry Hedge** (1805–1890) was an avid member of the emerging movement of new thinking that soon would be called Transcendentalism. As a boy, he had studied in Germany for four years prior to entering Harvard and as a result was not only fluent in German but also comfortable with the new ideas emerging from the German philosophers Johann Gottlieb Fichte (1762–1814) and Friedrich Wilhelm Joseph von Schelling (1775–1854). Brilliant and assertive in character, Hedge did not hesitate to proclaim the new thinking, even as he prepared for the ministry and took his place in the pulpits of New England.

In 1833, Hedge published an article in the *Christian Examiner* entitled "Coleridge's Literary Character." As we learn from Richardson, this article would be a powerful influence upon Emerson, who called it "a living, leaping logos," strong words for an article.[8] In it, Hedge made the distinction between the empiricists and the idealists so obvious, so clear and compelling, that it must have drawn Emerson right out of his chair.

> If Fichte confined himself too exclusively to the subjective, Schelling on the other hand treats principally of the object, and endeavors to show that *the outward world is of the same essence as the thinking mind, both being different manifestations of the same divine principle* [emphasis added]. He is the ontologist of the Kantian school. All knowledge, according to him, consists in an agreement between an object and a subject. In all science, therefore, there are these two elements or poles, subject and object, or nature and intelligence; and corresponding to these poles there are two fundamental sciences, the one beginning with nature and proceeding upward to intelligence and the other beginning with intelligence and ending in nature. The first is natural philosophy, the second transcendental philosophy.[9]

In this article, for the first time, Hedge laid out the *essentialist* position at its very core and gave the movement its language and persuasive power. As Richardson has it, "If there is a single moment after which American transcendentalism can be said to exist, it is when Emerson read Hedge's manifesto."[10]

Into this growing debate about the nature of human understanding and modes of knowing stepped **Amos Bronson Alcott,** although somewhat late to the scene. He did not finally settle in the Boston/Concord area until 1834, coming in that year from Connecticut to open the Temple School in Boston. That said, however, it was in his role as teacher that Alcott made his mark among many of those in the Boston community who were searching for new direction and inspiration. Fortunately, we have a record of actual classroom discussions, or "conversations," as Alcott called his lessons, in *How Like an Angel Came I Down: Conversations with Children on the Gospels.*

This record of Alcott's Temple School, as recorded by Elizabeth Peabody from 1835 to 1837, reveals principles that astonish and help us to understand why Alcott's unrecorded conversations with Emerson must have been influential. The "Original Author's Preface" to Alcott's book forms part of the sources to follow, but the remark of one five-year-old may have said it best, in a comment recorded by Peabody. The boy said to his teacher, "Oh, Mr. Alcott, I never knew I had a mind until I came to this school!"

During the years in which the Temple School struggled to stay open and viable, Alcott made frequent trips out to Concord to meet and visit with Emerson. The two shared walks and deep conversations. At some point Alcott lent Emerson his journal, which was the source for "Orphic Sayings." Entries such as "Solitude" mark Alcott as influential in the movement, the seeds of which in Emerson's hands would soon blossom. Alcott wrote, "Solitude is Wisdom's school. Attend then the lessons of your own soul; become a pupil of the wise God within you, for by his tuitions alone shall you grow into the knowledge and stature of the deities. The seraphs descend from heaven, in the solitudes of meditation, in the stillness of prayer."

In *Nature*, published anonymously in 1836, Emerson would close this founding document with a section in quotation marks, credited to his "Orphic Poet." Many scholars and biographers attribute this section to Alcott, although none of the language appears in the latter's journals. But the sense of the passage is Alcott's alone, a far-reaching, lofty affirmation of spiritual principles.

Man is the dwarf of himself. Once he was permeated and dissolved by spirit. He filled nature with his overflowing currents. Out from him sprang the sun and moon; from man, the sun; from woman, the moon. The laws of his mind, the periods of his actions externized themselves into day and night, into the year and the seasons. But, having made for himself this huge shell, his waters retired; he no longer fills the veins and veinlets; he is shrunk to a drop. He sees, that the structure still fits him, but fits him colossally. Say, rather, once it fitted him, now it corresponds to him from far and on high. He adores timidly his own work. Now is man the follower of the sun, and woman the follower of the moon. Yet sometimes he starts in his slumber, and wonders at himself and his house, and muses strangely at the resemblance betwixt him and it. He perceives that if his law is still paramount, if still he have elemental power, if his word is sterling yet in nature, it is not conscious power, it is not inferior but superior to his will. It is Instinct." Thus my Orphic poet sang.[11]

The first important historical analysis of Transcendentalism was published in 1876 by Octavius Brooks Frothingham, important because it was written while most of the major figures were still alive and could testify as to sources and pivotal moments. Frothingham devotes a chapter to Alcott entitled "The Mystic" and credits Alcott with being the leader of the movement before Emerson took center stage. He also credits Alcott with keeping Transcendentalism in the company of the mystics, albeit marginally, saying that Alcott was "a thinker, interior, solitary, deeply conversant with the secrets of his own mind."[12]

We shall have more to say about Emerson's contribution in "Individual Voices," but he must also be considered a primary source for the movement. Emerson published *Nature* in 1836 and as a result would immediately be regarded as the leader, if not founder, of Transcendentalism. As the passages from the introduction and Chapter 1 demonstrate, Emerson's willingness to offer testimony to his own revelatory experience, flying as it did in the face of traditional authority, marked him as both courageous to his supporters and foolhardy to his detractors. Specifically, it was the "transparent eyeball" experience from Chapter 1 of *Nature* that aligned him with Alcott and finally separated him from the carefully circumscribed doctrines of Unitarianism.

I have referred elsewhere to this seminal experience in Emerson's spiritual life as a "gnostic influx."[13] The experience took place on or about March 19, 1835, and it was recorded in his journal in almost the exact form as it appears in *Nature*. The key to the experience was its startling withdrawal of personal ego in the presence of the moment—in other words, its transparency of vision.

Standing on the bare ground,—my head bathed by the blithe air, and uplifted into infinite space,—all mean egotism vanishes. I become a transparent eye-ball; I am nothing; I see all; the currents of the Universal Being circulate through me; I am part or particle of God.[14]

As is evident throughout his work, this single moment of dissolving into the cosmos with its divine infusion would inspire Emerson for the rest of his life. He did not need a repeat of the moment, nor did he ever experience anything as intense. It was enough that he could penetrate the veil of appearances and find the ground of being in that chill November twilight. Keys to the experience were its freedom from personal claim and its total surprise. It did not take place while in prayer, or in contemplation or reflection upon a sacred text. He was simply walking along, as he said, "without having in my thoughts any occurrence of special good fortune." The reflection upon the experience closes with the sentence, "I am glad to the brink of fear." The juxtaposition of joy and fear is telling. Emerson was not willing to play it safe in matters of revelation. He was not content to take at second hand the "tuitions" of others, but required an intuition of his own. That he was willing to pass it on as testimony exposed him to the ridicule of the orthodox thinkers, even the Boston newspaper cartoonists of the day, who pictured Emerson as a top-hatted, spider-legged, strolling eyeball.

The final primary source of the movement, making New England Transcendentalism unique in its imagery and eloquence, was the presence and human relationship to nature itself, in particular, as seen by these writers, nature as a manifestation of consciousness. By the early nineteenth century in and around Boston, nature was no longer perceived as that dark, hellish realm of danger and temptation characteristic of the Puritan past. The once forbidding interior was gradually being opened to travel, farming, and trade. Concord, the nation's first inland community, was a leader in such development.

By 1820 Boston was a city of forty thousand people and would grow to sixty thousand through the next decade. For Emerson, who was born and schooled in Boston but spent many happy hours in the near wilderness of Concord, city life was too distracting and much too aggressively commercial. He and his friends began to think of this new country existence as more conducive to the examined life. Here, for example, is a passage from his essay "Nature":

> At the gates of the forest, the surprised man of the world is forced to leave his city estimates of great and small, wise and foolish. The knapsack of custom falls off his back with the first step he makes into these precincts. Here is sanctity which shames our religions, and reality which discredits our heroes. . . . Here no history, or church, or state, is interpolated on the divine sky and the immortal year. How easily we might walk onward into the opening landscape, absorbed by new pictures, and by thoughts fast succeeding each other, until by degrees the recollection of home was crowded out of the mind, all memory obliterated by the tyranny of the present, and we were led in triumph by nature.

Emerson lists here the central themes of Transcendentalism: the sanctity of nature as against the duality and illusions of ordinary (city) life, with its customary accretions; and the falling away of time and distraction to reveal, in solitude, the welcome and revelatory "tyranny of the present."

This view of nature stood in stark contrast to the forbidding forests of Puritan New England, particularly as seen in Nathaniel Hawthorne's *The Scarlet Letter.* Hawthorne was a contemporary and sometime neighbor of the Emersons in Concord, but he, like Marsh, avoided what he called the extremes of the Emerson circle. His darker view found sustenance in the Salem of the 1650s and included a view of nature as a moral wilderness, a place where temptations of all kinds were set free from the restraints of church and society. It was under the dark cover of the forest that Hester Prynne and Arthur Dimmesdale committed adultery, and although Hawthorne gives their love a certain moral sanction in the novel, he also sees, as did Marsh, the overwhelming power of society's moral constraints.

The Transcendentalists did not experience such an aversion. Their expressions of freedom and personal instinct were generally framed in opposition to societal restraints. Instead, assuming a conscious source, they put forward a new vision of the moral law in harmony with natural law. Their conviction, drawn from Platonic sources, was that if society's laws are found to be in conflict with natural law, then they have no sanction. Thoreau's "Civil Disobedience" is built on this principle and reflects the Greek notion that natural law (*physis*) must harmonize with society's law (*nomos*) in order to establish a just society.

Although the early writing of the Transcendentalists tended to find expression in traditional theological language, all that changed when Emerson published *Nature* in 1836. Here at last, drawn from the European and American sources, was the connection between the laws of nature and the laws of the human mind.

Emerson had found a way, through the imagery of the natural world, to harmonize the worlds of religion, science, culture, and literature, with the human mind being both the source and the means of unification. It would be the touchstone of the movement.

Finally, the selection of the following materials, especially those involving the primary sources and some of the minor figures in the movement, illustrates the principle of *essentialism,* not only in that term's metaphysical meaning of asserting the preeminence of essence over existence, but also in its more literary sense of stripping away nonessential elements to concentrate on main points. Thus, the selections that follow will not generally include supportive arguments, illustrations of main points, or contextual explanations. Readers interested in context are referred to the selected bibliography of full texts.

PRIMARY TEXTS

For the writings of Sampson Reed, James Marsh, and Samuel Taylor Coleridge, in particular, the excerpts from their founding documents have been selected for their immediate relevance to the later thinking and work of the major figures represented in the movement. In the cases of Alcott and Emerson, selections are based on early influential work.

SAMPSON REED

The following are passages from *Observations on the Growth of the Mind,* published in Boston in 1826. Readers interested in the full text of the pamphlet may find it in Joel Myerson's comprehensive anthology *Transcendentalism.*

While men have been speculating concerning their own powers, the sure but secret influence of revelation has been gradually changing the moral and intellectual character of the world, and the ground on which they were standing has passed from under them, almost while their words were in their mouths. The powers of the mind are most intimately connected with the subjects by which they were occupied. We cannot think of the will without feeling, of the understanding without thought, or of the imagination without something like poetry.

Is, then, everything that relates to the immortal part of men fleeting and evanescent, while the laws of physical nature remain unaltered? Do things become changeable as we approach the immutable and the eternal? Far otherwise. The laws of the mind are in themselves as fixed and perfect as the laws of matter; but they are laws from which we have wandered. There is a philosophy of the mind, founded not on the aspect it presents in any part or in any period of the world, but on its immutable relations to its first cause; a philosophy equally applicable to man, before or after he has passed the valley of the shadow of death; not dependent on time or place, but immortal as its subject. The light of this philosophy has begun to beam faintly on the world, and mankind will yet see their own moral and intellectual nature by the light of revelation, as it shines through the moral and intellectual character it shall have itself created.

Eternity is to the mind what time is to nature. We attain a perception of it, by regarding all the operations in the world within us, as they exist in relation to their first cause; for in doing this, they are seen to partake somewhat of the nature of that Being on whom they depend. We make no approaches to a conception of it, by heaping day upon day or year upon year. This is merely an accumulation of time; and we might as well attempt to convey an idea of mental greatness by that of actual space, as to communicate a conception of eternity by years or thousands of years. Mind and matter are not more distinct from each other than their properties; and by an attempt to embrace all time, we are actually farther from an approach to eternity than when we confine ourselves to a single instant; because we merely collect the largest possible amount of natural changes, whereas that which is eternal approaches that which is immutable.

It is natural for the mature mind to ask the cause of things. It is unsatisfied when it does not find one, and can hardly exclude the thought of that Being, from whom all things exist. When therefore we have gone beyond the circle of youthful knowledge, and found a phenomenon in nature, which in its insulated state fills us with the admiration of God; let us beware how we quench this feeling. Let us rather transfer something of this admiration to those phenomena of the same class, which have not hitherto directed our minds beyond the fact of their actual existence.

The science of mind itself will be the effect of its own development. This is merely an attendant consciousness, which the mind possesses, of the growth of its own powers; and therefore, it would seem, need not be made a distinct object of study. Thus the power of reason may be perceptively developed by the study pf the demonstrative sciences. As it is developed, the pupil becomes conscious of its existence and its use.

The body and the mind should grow together, and form the sound and perfect man, whose understanding may be almost measured by its stature. The mind will see itself in what it loves and is able to accomplish. Its own works will be its mirror; and when it is present in the natural world, feeling the same spirit which gives life to every object by which it is surrounded, in its very union with nature it will catch a glimpse of itself, like that of pristine beauty united with innocence, at her own native fountain.

Natural philosophy seems almost essential to an enlightened independence of thought and action. A man may lean upon others, and be so well supported by an equal pressure in all directions, as to be apparently dependent on no one; but his independence is apt to degenerate into obstinacy, or betray itself in weakness, unless his mind is fixed on this unchanging basis. A knowledge of the world may give currency to his sentiments, and plausibility to his manners; but it is more frequently a knowledge of *the world* that gives light to the path, and stability to the purpose.

It belongs to the true poet to feel this [creative spirit of God], and to be governed by it; to be raised above the senses; to live and breathe in the inward efforts of things; to feel the power of creation, even before he sees the effect; to witness the innocence and smiles of nature's infancy, not by extending the imagination back to chaos, but by raising the soul to nature's origin. The true poetic spirit, so far from misleading any, is the strongest bulwark against deception. It is the soul of science.

The state of poetry has always indicated the state of science and religion. The gods are hardly missed more, when removed from the temples of the ancients, than they are when taken from their poetry; or than theory is, when taken from their philosophy.

As the philosophy connected with the natural world is that in which the mind may take root, by which it may possess an independence worthy a being whose eternal destiny is in his own hands—so the moral and civil institutions, the actual condition of society, is the atmosphere which surrounds and protects it; in which it sends forth its branches and bears fruit.

Every individual also possesses peculiar powers, which should be brought to bear on society in the duties best fitted to receive them. The highest degree of cultivation of which the mind of any one is capable, consists in the most perfect development of that peculiar organization and, by a life entirely governed by the commandments of God, to leave on the duties we are called on to perform the full impress of our real characters. Let a man's ambition to be great disappear in a willingness to be what he is; then he may fill a high place without pride, or a low one without dejection. As our desires become more and more concentrated to those objects which correspond to the peculiar organization of our minds, we shall have a foretaste of that which is coming, in those internal tendencies of which we are conscious.

JAMES MARSH

What follows is the preface from the American edition (1840) of *Aids to Reflection* by Samuel Taylor Coleridge. The selection below focuses attention solely on the essential point of the distinction between the words *understanding* and *reason,* a distinction made clear by Coleridge and carried forward by the Transcendentalists, particularly Emerson, in their theories of the mind and its relation to revelation.

Now it is not too much to say, that most men, and even a large proportion of educated men, do not reflect sufficiently upon their own inward being, upon the constituent laws of their own understanding, upon the mysterious powers and agencies of reason, and conscience, and will, to apprehend with much distinctness the objects to be named, or of course to refer the names with correctness to their several objects.

I will merely observe that the key to his [Coleridge's] system will be found in the distinctions, which he makes and illustrates between *nature* and *free-will,* and between the *understanding* and *reason.* . . . It must have been observed by the reader of the foregoing pages, that I have used several words, especially understanding and reason, in a sense somewhat diverse from their present acceptation; and the occasion of this I suppose would be partly understood from my having already directed the attention of the reader to the distinction exhibited between these two words in the Work [*Aids to Reflection*], and from the remarks made on the ambiguity of the word "reason" in its common use.

Nor am I alone in this view. . . . A literary friend, whose opinion on this subject would be valued by all who know the soundness of his scholarship, says, in a letter just now received,—"if you can once get the attention of thinking men fixed on this distinction between the reason and the understanding, you will have done enough to reward the labor of a life. As prominent a place as he holds it in the writings of Coleridge, he seems to me far enough from making too much of it." No person of serious and philosophical mind, I am confident, can reflect upon the subject, enough to understand it in its various aspects, without arriving at the same views of the importance of the distinction, whatever may be his conviction with regard to its truth.

In the ascending series of powers, enumerated by Milton, with so much philosophical truth, as well as beauty of language, in the fifth book of Paradise Lost, he mentions,

> *Fancy and understanding, whence the soul*
> *Reason receives. And reason is her being,*
> *Discursive or intuitive.*

But the highest power here, that which is the being of the soul, considered as any thing differing in kind from the *understanding,* has no place in our popular metaphysics. Thus, we have only the understanding, "the faculty of judging according to sense," a faculty of abstracting and generalizing, of contrivance and forecast, as the highest of our intellectual powers; and this we are expressly taught belongs to us in common with brutes. Nay, these views of our essential being, consequences and all, are adopted by men, whom one would suppose religion, if not philosophy, should have taught their utter inadequateness to the true and essential constituents of our humanity.

In this brief excerpt from the actual text of *Aids to Reflection,* Coleridge gives a clear outline of the relationship of the reasoning faculty and the understanding faculty in mind. It was this distinction that fed into the notion of infinitude developed later by Emerson.

1. Understanding is discursive.
2. The understanding in all its judgments refers to some other faculty as its ultimate authority.
3. Understanding is the faculty of reflection.

1. Reason is fixed.
2. The reason in all its decision appeals to itself as the ground and substance of their truth.
3. Reason of contemplation. Reason is much nearer to sense than to understanding: for reason is a direct aspect of truth, an inward beholding, having a similar relation to the untellable as spiritual, as sense has to the material or phenomenal.

Understanding is discursive; Reason is fixed. The Understanding in all its judgments refers to some other faculty as its ultimate authority; The Reason in all its decisions appeals to itself as the ground and substance of their truth. Understanding is the faculty of reflection; Reason [the faculty] of contemplation. Reason is much nearer to Sense than to Understanding: for Reason is a direct aspect of truth, an inward beholding, having a similar relation to the intelligible or spiritual, as Sense has to the material or phenomenal. . . . The Understanding then, considered exclusively as an organ of human intelligence, is the faculty by which we reflect and generalize. . . . The Understanding is truly and accurately defined in the words of Leighton and Kant, a faculty judging according to sense . . . the speculative

Reason,—that is, the reason considered abstractedly as an intellective power—we call it "the source of necessary and universal principles, according to which the notices of the senses are either affirmed or denied"; or describe it as "the power by which we are enabled to draw from particular and contingent appearances universal and necessary conclusions." . . . The dependence of the Understanding on the representations of the senses, and its consequent posteriority thereto, as contrasted with the independence and antecedency of Reason, are strikingly exemplified in the Ptolemaic system—that truly wonderful product and highest boast of the faculty, judging according to the senses—compared with the Newtonian, as the offspring of a yet higher power, arranging, correcting, and annulling the representations of the senses according to its own inherent laws and constitutive ideas.

On the contrary, reason is the power of universal and necessary convictions, the source and substance of truths above sense, and having their evidence in themselves. Its presence is always marked by the necessity of the position affirmed: this necessity being conditional, when a truth of reason is applied to facts of experience, or to the rules and maxims of the understanding; but absolute, when the subject matter is itself the growth or offspring of reason. Hence arises a distinction in reason itself, derived from the different mode of applying it, and from the objects to which it is directed: accordingly as we consider one and the same gift, now as the ground of formal principles, and now as the origin of ideas. Contemplated distinctively in reference to formal (or abstract) truth, it is the speculative reason; but in reference to actual (or moral) truth, as the fountain of ideas and the light of the conscience, we name it the practical reason. Whenever by self-subjection to this universal light, the will of the individual, the particular will has become a will of reason, the man is regenerative: and reason is then the spirit of the regenerated man, whereby the person is capable of a quickening inter-communion with the Divine Spirit.

AMOS BRONSON ALCOTT

What follows are early journal entries,[15] the first twelve "Orphic Sayings," and the "Original Editor's Preface" from *How Like an Angel Came I Down*. Emerson read these early journals and was influenced by them in both substance and style. His own eloquence, however, transformed Alcott into a sharper, more trenchant affirmation.

ALCOTT'S EARLY JOURNALS

Notes on Religion (October 5, 1828)
I am dissatisfied with the general preaching of any sect of men, and with the individuals of any sect. The general style of preaching, as regards thought and manner, among the Unitarians approaches nearer my views of correct preaching than that of any other class, but even this, it seems to me, is very objectionable. There is too much merely doctrinal, too little of practical thought. Hearers are returned home little better prepared, in too many instances, for the intelligent performance of their duties. Religion, after all, is not made

a sufficiently rational, spontaneous, and social affair. Duties is too much involved in beliefs, in theory, in form, rather than in practice, in intelligent feeling and action. The morality of the pulpit is not sufficiently adapted to that of everyday life—to teach men how to die rather than how to live, to present the felicities of another life as objects of attainment rather than those of the present. It takes the thoughts of men too far from themselves—to heaven, rather than to the concerns of earth given us by our great Employer.

Notes on Philosophy (May 1833)

Modern philosophy has widely departed from the genius of the ancient school. The living spirit has departed from it, and left it dead and corrupt mass of material elements. That [ancient] had intercommunion with the invisible and the infinite; this [modern] is limited to the consideration of the finite and visible, and is incompetent to the investigation of primary causes and ultimate laws. It stops at secondary causes and can penetrate no deeper. It limits and circumscribes the infinite by the frail and powerless energies of the finite. It shuts God from the universe, and, carried to its legitimate issues, results in Pantheism—building up on an inconceivable basis the whole fabrick of religion, which it must assume as independent of man and nature. It makes of exterior nature a self-existent substance, and sees not in the laws and vicissitudes of things the movement of Spirit.

These illusions, which never had much influence over my own mind, have all been swept away by the Platonic theory, and I see clearly what before was obscured by the gloss of exterior matter: Spirit all in all—matter its form and shadow.

Notes on the Self (April 27, 1834)

I have so long lived an inward, reflective life that the relations of external things to my temporal prosperity have been almost lost sight of. I am not perhaps sufficiently inclined to yield to the dictates of earthly prudence. I cling too closely to the ideal to take the necessary advantage of the practical, and my wife and children suffer from this neglect. I may not sympathize with a true spirit in the deprivations to which this course subjects them. Disinclined from making much of outward success, I may seem unkind, indifferent, improvident.

But this course seems to me the only one that I can pursue in justice to all relations and purposes in life. I have set out in an attempt to find the truths of my own nature, to explain and embody them in life, in education. Sacrifices must be made to the spirit of the age. With a new purpose, I must expect difficulties which are not thrown in the way of those who pass on unopposingly in the current stream of things. In proportion to the value of the ends which I aim at must be the sacrifices that I make, the obstacles to encounter, and the distance of the day when success will crown my efforts.

Notes on Nature (June 12, 1834)

And the name of that chamber was "Peace."
Pilgrim's Progress

This sentence keeps chiming in my ears as I sit at my desk this morning in my chamber, the window of which opens to the sun-rising, and before me are the trees clad in the rich foliage of the season—tho morning breese scarcely stirring their leaves, and the sunlight settling in no unquiet repose on the sloping rooftops of the houses around me. The aspect of nature at this hour is that of peace and refreshing quiet. The mind, invigorated by the visitations of the night, is returned with transparent vision to the objects of earth and breathes in the spirit of the scene. Peace and quietness are impressed upon it from without; it drinks in the natural scenery and finds growing up, in the ideal landscape within, fresher and fresher objects—waving trees, clad in green, calmer sunlight. The chamber within is tenanted by the glad spirit of "Peace."

FROM "ORPHIC SAYINGS"

As printed in the Transcendentalist magazine *The Dial.* These entries are both spiritual definitions and inspired affirmations. Sometimes eloquent but too frequently pretentious in style, they were an easy target for parody, sometimes hurtfully so after they appeared in print.

I. SPIRIT.

Listen divinely to the sibyl within thee, saith the Spirit, and write thou her words. For now is thine intellect a worshipper of the Holy Ghost; now thy life is mystic—thy words marvels—and thine appeal to the total sense of man—a nature to the soul.

1. Nature.

Nature bares never her bones; clothed in her own chaste

rhetoric of flesh and blood—of color and feature, she is elegant and fair to the sense. And thus, O Philosopher, Poet, Prophet, be thy words—thy Scriptures;—thy thought, like Pallas, shaped bold and comely from thy brain—like Venus, formed quick from thy side—mystic as Memnon—melodious as the lyre of Orpheus.

2. Immanence.

There is neither void in nature, nor death in spirit,—all is vital, nothing Godless. Both guilt in the soul and pain in the flesh, affirm the divine ubiquity in the all of being. Shadow apes substance, privation fullness; and nature in atom and whole, in planet and firmament, is charged with the present Deity.

3. Incarnation.

Nature is quick with spirit. In eternal systole and diastole, the living tides course gladly along, incarnating organ and vessel in their mystic flow. Let her pulsations for a moment pause on their errands, and creation's self ebbs instantly into chaos and invisibility again. The visible world is the extremest wave of that spiritual flood, whose flux is life, whose reflux death, efflux thought, and conflux light. Organization is the confine of incarnation,—body the atomy of God.

4. Faith.

Sense beholds life never,—death always. For nature is but the fair corpse of spirit, and sense her tomb. Philosophy holds her torch while science dissects the seemly carcase. 'Tis faith unseals the sepulchres, and gives the risen Godhead to the soul's embrace. Blessed is he, who without sense believeth,—for already is he resurrect and immortal!

5. Unbelief.

Impious faith! witless philosophy! prisoning God in the head, to gauge his volume or sound his depths, by admeasurements of brain. Know, man of skulls! that the soul builds her statue perpetually from the dust, and, from within, the spiritual potter globes this golden bowl on which thy sacrilegious finger is laid. Be wise, fool! and divine cerebral qualities from spiritual laws, and predict organizations from character.

6. Oracle.

Believe, youth, despite all temptations, the oracle of deity in your own bosom. 'Tis the breath of God's revelations,— the respiration of the Holy Ghost in your breast. Be faithful, not infidel, to its intuitions,—quench never its spirit,—dwell ever in its omniscience. So shall your soul be filled with light, and God be an indwelling fact,—a presence in the depths of your being.

7. Heroism.

Great is the man whom his age despises. For transcendent excellence is purchased through the obloquy of contemporaries; and shame is the gate to the temple of renown. The heroism honored of God, and the gratitude of mankind, achieves its marvels in the shades of life, remote from the babble of crowds.

8. Desert.

Praise and blame as little belong to the righteous as to God. Virtue transcends desert—as the sun by day, as heat during frosts. Its light and warmth are its essence, cheering alike the wilderness, the fields, and fire-sides of men,—the cope of heaven, and the bowels of the earth.

9. Patience.

Be great even in your leisures; making, accepting, opportunities, and doing lovingly your work at the first or eleventh hour, even as God has need of you. Transcend all occasions; exhausted, overborne, by none. Wisdom waits with a long patience; nor working, nor idling with men and times; but living and being in eternity with God. Great designs demand ages for consummation, and Gods are coadjutors in their accomplishment. Patience is king of opportunity and times.

10. Solitude.

Solitude is Wisdom's school. Attend then the lessons of your own soul; become a pupil of the wise God within you, for by his tuitions alone shall you grow into the knowledge and stature of the deities. The seraphs descend from heaven, in the solitudes of meditation, in the stillness of prayer.

11. Atonement.

All sin is original,—there is none other; and so all atonement for sin. God's method is neither mediatorial nor vicarious; and the soul is nor saved nor judged by proxy,—she saves or dooms herself. Piety is unconscious, vascular, vital,—like breathing it IS, and is because it is. None can respire for another, none sin or atone for another's sin. Redemption is a personal, private act.

12. Blessedness.

Blessedness consists in perfect willingness. It is above all conflict. It is serenity, triumph, beatitude. It transcends choice. It is one with the divine Will, and a partaker of his nature and tendency. There is struggle and choice only with the wilful. The saints are elect in perfect obedience, and enact God's decrees.

ALCOTT'S ORIGINAL AUTHOR'S PREFACE TO
CONVERSATIONS WITH CHILDREN

The work now presented to the reader, forms the introduction to a course of conversations with children, on the Life of Christ, as recorded in the Gospels. It is the Record of an attempt to unfold the Idea of Spirit from the Consciousness of Childhood; and to trace its Intellectual and Corporeal Relations; its Temptations and Disciplines; its Struggles and Conquests, while in the Flesh. To this end, the character of Jesus has been presented to the consideration of children, as the brightest Symbol of Spirit; and they have been encouraged to express their views regarding it. The Conductor of these conversations has reverently explored their consciousness, for the testimony which it might furnish in favor of the truth of Christianity,

Assuming as a fact the spiritual integrity of the young mind, he was desirous of placing under the inspection of children, a character so much in conformity with their own, as that of Jesus of Nazareth. He believed that children would as readily apprehend the divine beauty of this character, when rightly presented, as adults. He even hoped that, through their simple consciousness, the Divine Idea of a Man, as Imaged in Jesus, yet almost lost to the world, might be revived in the mind of adults, who might thus be recalled into the spiritual kingdom. These views, confirmed by long intimacy with the young, as well as by the tendency of his own mind to regard the bright visions of childhood, as the promise of the soul's future blessedness; as the loadstar to conduct it through this terrestrial Life, led him to undertake this enterprise, and to prosecute it with a deep and kindling interest, which he feels will continue unabated to its close.

The Editor will not, meanwhile, conceal the fact, that it is with no little solicitude that he ventures these documents before the eye of others. He feels that his book should be studied in Simplicity. It is, in no small measure, the production of children. It is a record of their consciousness; a natural history of the undepraved spirit. It is the testimony of unspoiled natures to the spiritual purity of Jesus. It is a revelation of the Divinity in the soul of childhood. Like the Sacred volume—on which it is, indeed, a juvenile commentary—of which it is an interpretation, it cannot be at once, apprehended in all its bearings, and find its true value.

There may be those, however, who, unconscious of its worth, shall avail themselves of the statements, views, and speculations, which it contains, to the detriment of religion and humanity; not perceiving, that it is a work, intended rather to awaken thought; enkindle feeling; and quicken to duty; than to settle opinions, or promulgate sentiments of any kind. Whoever shall find its significance, will scarce treat with disrespect these products of the sacred being of childhood. For childhood utters sage things, worthy of all note; and he who scoffs at its improvisations, or perverts its simple sayings, proves the corruption of his own being, and his want of reverence for the Good, the Beautiful, the True, and the Holy. He beholds not the Face of the Heavenly Father.

It has been a main purpose of the Conductor of these conversations, to tempt forth, by appropriate questions, the cherished sentiments of the children on the subjects presented to their consideration. It was no part of his intention to bring forward, except by necessary implication, his own favorite opinions as a means of biassing, in the smallest degree, the judgments and decisions of the children. He wished to inculcate only what was the universal product of our common nature. He endeavoured to avoid dogmatizing. He was desirous of gathering the sentiments of the little circle, in which it is his pleasure and privilege to move as teacher and friend. He believed that Christianity was in Childhood, and he sought the readiest and simplest means to unfold it, and bring it into the light of day.

That he has withheld his own sentiments from the children in all instances, he can scarce hope. It was next to impossible. He has doubtless led them, in some instances, by the tenor of his questions, and his manner of disposing of replies, to the adoption or rejection of sentiments, foreign to their nature. But he believes that he has seldom erred in this way. He preferred to become the simple Analyst of the consciousness of the children, and, having no opinions of his own to establish against their common convictions, he treated with reverence whatever he found within it, deeming it, when spontaneous, a revelation of the same Divinity, as was Jesus.

He is aware that the work which he has assumed is one of great difficulty. He feels that it is not easy to ascertain the precise state of a child's mind. He knows that much of what a child utters has been received from others, that language is an uncertain organ in his use; that he often endows words with his own significance; that he is liable to mistake the phenomenon of his own consciousness; and moreover, that his scanty vocabulary often leaves him without the means of revealing himself. Still some certainty is attainable. For a child can be trusted when urged to ingenuous expression; and when all temptations to deceive are withdrawn. A wise and sympathizing observer will readily distinguish the real from the assumed; penetrate through all the varying phases of expression, and do him justice.

Yet, while so little is done to guard children against servile imitation, by a wise training of their minds to original thought, we are in danger of not giving them credit for what is their own. So little confidence, indeed, do we place in their statements, and so imitative do we deem them, that, when a wise saying chances to drop from their lips, instead of regarding it, as it of right should be, the product of their own minds, we seek its origin among adults, as if it must of necessity spring from this source alone. We greatly underrate the genius of children. We do not apprehend the inward power, that but awaits the genial touch, to be quickened into life. The art of tempting this forth we have scarce attained. We have outlived our own simple consciousness, and have thus lost our power of apprehending them. We have yet to learn, that Wisdom and Holiness are of no Age; that they preexist, separate from time, and are the possession of Childhood, not less than of later years; that they, indeed, often appear in fresher features, in the earlier seasons of life, than in physical maturity. In Man they are often quenched by the vulgar aims of the corporeal life.

To a child, all questions touching the Soul are deeply interesting. He loves his own consciousness. It is a charmed world to him. As yet he has not been drawn out of it by the seductions of the propensities; nor is he beguiled by the illusions of his external senses. And were he assisted in the study and discipline of it, by those who could meet his wants, and on whom he could rely, his spiritual acquirements would keep pace with his years, and he would grow up wise in the mysteries of the spiritual kingdom. The Divine Idea of a Man, the vision of Self-Perfection, would live in his consciousness; instead of being, as now, pushed aside by the intrusive images, and vulgar claims, of unhallowed appetite and desire. Christ would be formed in the Soul the Hope of Immortality.

In the original copy of this record, the names of the speakers were preserved, as necessary to identify their different views and statements. It is feared that some persons may regret the insertion of these in the printed volume, from a regard to the effect on the speakers themselves. Yet to have used assumed names would have impaired the identity of the record, and have diminished its value, of course, as an historical fact. No serious evils, it is believed can arise from retaining them. The children expressed themselves in simplicity; there is nothing in their remarks, to flatter their vanity; and they have no desire to see their names in print. The Editor would regret extremely, to be the means of wounding the feelings of those of his patrons, who have expressed their sympathy with his views, and who, amid much to try their faith in the practicability of his attempt to renovate education, have continued their children under his care. Much less, would he wantonly do ought to injure, in the slightest degree, that simplicity and meekness, which he has sought to cherish in those, for whose spiritual and intellectual culture, these conversations were primarily intended.

The Editor would remark, in conclusion, that he deems

his labors valuable, not only to those children, who were present at these conversations, and to the general reader, but he ventures to hope that they will commend themselves, also, to those parents and teachers, who deem the spiritual growth and discipline of those committed to their care, of unspeakable and primary importance. He trusts that he has given, in these specimens of his intercourse with children, a model, not unworthy of imitation, of the simplest and readiest mode of presenting religious truth to the young. He believes that he has shed some light over the path of Human Culture. He feels, that for children, if not for adults, he has delineated, and in a form which they can apprehend, the Divine Life of Jesus; and has urged upon them, through the mouths of his little ones, considerations and motives, fitted to inspire them with the noble ambition to strive to imitate his Example.

RALPH WALDO EMERSON

The following selections are from the introduction and Chapter 1 of Emerson's essay *Nature,* written in 1836.

INTRODUCTION

Our age is retrospective. It builds the sepulchres of the fathers. It writes biographies, histories, and criticism. The foregoing generations beheld God and nature face to face; we, through their eyes. Why should not we also enjoy an original relation to the universe? Why should not we have a poetry and philosophy of insight and not of tradition, and a religion by revelation to us, and not the history of theirs? Embosomed for a season in nature, whose floods of life stream around and through us, and invite us by the powers they supply, to action proportioned to nature, why should we grope among the dry bones of the past, or put the living generation into masquerade out of its faded wardrobe? The sun shines to-day also. There is more wool and flax in the fields. There are new lands, new men, new thoughts. Let us demand our own works and laws and worship.

Undoubtedly we have no questions to ask which are unanswerable. We must trust the perfection of the creation so far, as to believe that whatever curiosity the order of things has awakened in our minds, the order of things can satisfy. Every man's condition is a solution in hieroglyphic to those inquiries he would put. He acts it as life, before he apprehends it as truth. In like manner, nature is already, in its forms and tendencies, describing its own design. Let us interrogate the great apparition, that shines so peacefully around us. Let us inquire, to what end is nature?

All science has one aim, namely, to find a theory of nature. We have theories of races and of functions, but scarcely yet a remote approach to an idea of creation. We are now so far from the road to truth, that religious teachers dispute and hate each other, and speculative men are esteemed unsound and frivolous. But to a sound judgment, the most abstract truth is the most practical. Whenever a true theory appears, it will be its own evidence. Its test is, that it will explain all phenomena. Now many are thought not only unexplained but inexplicable; as language, sleep, madness, dreams, beasts, sex.

Philosophically considered, the universe is composed of Nature and the Soul. Strictly speaking, therefore, all that is separate from us, all which Philosophy distinguishes as the NOT ME, that is, both nature and art, all other men and my own body, must be ranked under this name, NATURE. In enumerating the values of nature and casting up their sum, I shall use the word in both senses;—in its common and in its philosophical import. In inquiries so general as our present one, the inaccuracy is not material; no confusion of thought will occur. Nature, in the common sense, refers to essences unchanged by man; space, the air, the river, the leaf. Art is applied to the mixture of his will with the same things, as in a house, a canal, a statue, a picture. But his operations taken together are so insignificant, a little chipping, baking, patching, and washing, that in an impression so grand as that of the world on the human mind, they do not vary the result.

CHAPTER 1

To go into solitude, a man needs to retire as much from his chamber as from society. I am not solitary whilst I read and write, though nobody is with me. But if a man would be alone, let him look at the stars. The rays that come from those heavenly worlds, will separate between him and what he touches. One might think the atmosphere was made transparent with this design, to give man, in the heavenly bodies, the perpetual presence of the sublime. Seen in the streets of cities, how great they are! If the stars should appear one night in a thousand years, how would men believe and adore; and preserve for many generations the remembrance of the city of God which had been shown! But every night come out these envoys of beauty, and light the universe with their admonishing smile.

The stars awaken a certain reverence, because though always present, they are inaccessible; but all natural objects make a kindred impression, when the mind is open to their influence. Nature never wears a mean appearance. Neither does the wisest man extort her secret, and lose his curiosity by finding out all her perfection. Nature never became a toy to a wise spirit. The flowers, the animals, the mountains, reflected the wisdom of his best hour, as much as they had delighted the simplicity of his childhood. When we speak of nature in this manner, we have a distinct but most poetical sense in the mind. We mean the integrity of impression made by manifold natural objects. It is this which distinguishes the stick of timber of the wood-cutter, from the tree of the poet. The charming landscape which I saw this morning, is indubitably made up of some twenty or thirty farms. Miller owns this field, Locke that, and Manning the woodland beyond. But none of them owns the landscape. There is a property in the horizon which no man has but he whose eye can integrate all the parts, that is, the poet. This is the best part of these men's farms, yet to this their warranty-deeds give no title. To speak truly, few adult persons can see nature. Most persons do not see the sun. At least they have a very superficial seeing. The sun illuminates only the eye of the man, but shines into the eye and the heart of the child. The lover of nature is he whose inward and outward senses are still truly adjusted to each other; who has retained the spirit of infancy even into the era of manhood. His intercourse with heaven and earth, becomes part of his daily food. In the presence of nature, a wild delight runs through the man, in spite of real sorrows. Nature says,—he is my creature, and maugre all his impertinent griefs, he shall be glad with me. Not the sun or the summer alone, but every hour and season yields its tribute of delight; for every hour and change corresponds to and authorizes a different state of the mind, from breathless noon to grimmest midnight. Nature is a setting that fits equally well a comic or a mourning piece. In good health, the air is a cordial of incredible virtue. Crossing a bare common, in snow puddles, at twilight, under a clouded sky, without having in my thoughts any occurrence of special good fortune, I have enjoyed a perfect exhilaration. I am glad to the brink of fear. In the woods too, a man casts off his years, as the snake his slough, and at what period soever of life, is always a child. In the woods, is perpetual youth. Within these plantations of God, a decorum and sanctity reign, a perennial festival is dressed, and the guest sees not how he should tire of them in a thousand years. In the woods, we return to reason and faith. There I feel that nothing can befall me in life,—no disgrace, no calamity, (leaving me my eyes,) which nature cannot repair. Standing on the bare ground,—my head bathed by the blithe air, and uplifted into infinite space,—all mean egotism vanishes. I become a transparent eye-ball; I am nothing; I see all; the currents of the Universal Being circulate through me; I am part or particle of God. The name of the nearest friend sounds then foreign and accidental: to be brothers, to be acquaintances,—master or servant, is then a trifle and a disturbance. I am the lover of uncontained and immortal beauty. In the wilderness, I find something more dear and connate than in streets or villages. In the tranquil landscape, and especially in the distant line of the horizon, man beholds somewhat as beautiful as his own nature.

The greatest delight which the fields and woods minister, is the suggestion of an occult relation between man and the vegetable. I am not alone and unacknowledged. They nod to me, and I to them. The waving of the boughs in the storm, is new to me and old. It takes me by surprise, and yet is not unknown. Its effect is like that of a higher thought or a better emotion coming over me, when I deemed I was thinking justly or doing right.

Yet it is certain that the power to produce this delight, does not reside in nature, but in man, or in a harmony of both. It is necessary to use these pleasures with great temperance. For, nature is not always tricked in holiday attire, but the same scene which yesterday breathed perfume and glittered as for the frolic of the nymphs, is overspread with melancholy today. Nature always wears the colors of the spirit. To a man laboring under calamity, the heat of his own fire hath sadness in it. Then, there is a kind of contempt of the landscape felt by him who has just lost by death a dear friend. The sky is less grand as it shuts down over less worth in the population.

II

INDIVIDUAL
VOICES

INTRODUCTION
TO INDIVIDUAL VOICES

I n 1840, Emerson looked back at the previous decade and made the following entry in his journal:

> *In all my lectures, I have taught one doctrine, namely, the infinitude of the private man. This the people accept readily enough, & even with loud commendation, as long as I call the lecture, Art, or Politics; or Literature; or the Household; but the moment I call it Religion,—they are shocked, though it be only the application of the same truth which they receive everywhere else, to a new class of facts."*[16]

The mild frustration in this observation is but a gentle head-shaking wonder. He knew perfectly well the danger of applying the notion of human infinitude to religious matters. Indeed, in the parlors of conformist society in Boston, accusations of madness had been directed at the Transcendentalists for years, and the primary focus was this notion of "infinitude" within human nature. Rejection of the vast reaches of inner life was commonplace, even as it is today. As Emerson also said, "Tell men to study themselves and, for the most part, they find nothing less interesting."[17]

But Emerson's aim in asserting this vision of infinitude was at least in part designed to counteract the reductive skepticism of the realists and to affirm the essentialism of the Idealist philosophy. But even on this point, Emerson's company diverged, and they went their separate ways. Each held his or her own views on the matter of human capacity, although they were certainly united in their rejection of sense-based limitations.

Also, however, Emerson's journal entry creates a mild confusion in his own reference to religion. Too much has been made in the past that Transcendentalism was primarily a religious movement, and Emerson's comment lends credibility to that assessment. In actuality the movement was a spiritual one. The difference is crucial. That which is *religious* centers on form and doctrine. A religion requires a recognized body of communicants who, by definition, establish and practice a form of worship different from other gatherings of communicants. The word *spiritual*, as it will be used here, refers to something more subtle, animating, individual and universal. In spiritual thinking and practice, the relation between the individual and God, or the Divine Spirit or Absolute, is highly personal and not defined by ritualized devotions. By definition, then, a religious context is one in which a mediating structure is prescribed and accepted by the communicant. In a spiritual context, no such mediation is desired or required. Therefore, in the sense used here and implied in the term *essential*, Transcendentalism was a spiritual movement, not a religious one. The idea of a Transcendental Church, then, is an oxymoron.

In addition, many commentators and cultural historians have minimized the impact of Transcendentalism on the grounds of its brevity, seeing in it a minor blip on the cultural radar. However, seen as a spiritual movement in the light of the ancient traditions of the Perennial Philosophy, of which it was a part, Transcendentalism was and is a continuation of a way of seeing and being in the world. In that sense, Transcendentalism has never lapsed.

Every serious spiritual movement, of course, has its divisions and disruptions, and in its heyday, Transcendentalism seemed, paradoxically, more divisive than harmonizing. Its opponents focused on the divisive qualities, saying that these heretics and misfits contributed nothing, that they turned their backs on the needs of society, preferring the sanctuary of their garrets and haunts in the deep woods. True enough, Emerson admitted; solitude was, he said, "intrinsic and progressive." Only in this way could there be true enlargement of the mind and the spirit. "The infinitude of the private man" was the core of the teaching, and at least half its import lay in the term "private."

By way of perspective, Emerson made historical reference to the movement in his journal in July 1866. This entry describes, better than anything we could say from a greater distance, the way the Emerson circle took its life and did its work.

> *I think there was the mistake of a general belief at that time, that there was some concert of doctrinaires to establish certain opinions, & inaugurate some movement in literature, philosophy, & religion, of which the supposed conspirators were quite innocent; for there was no concert, & only here & there, two or three men or women who read & wrote, each alone, with unusual vivacity. Perhaps they only agree in having fallen*

upon Coleridge, Wordsworth, Goethe, & then upon Carlyle, with pleasure & sympathy. Otherwise, their education & reading were not marked, but had the American superficialness, & their studies were solitary. I suppose all of them were surprised at this rumor of a school or sect, & certainly at the name of Transcendentalism, which nobody knows who gave, or when it was first applied.

As these persons became, in the common chance of society, acquainted with each other, there resulted certainly strong friendships, which, of course, were exclusive in proportion to their heat, & perhaps those persons who were mutually the best friends were the most private, & had no ambition of publishing their letters, diaries or conversation. Such were Charles Newcomb, Sam G. Ward, & Caroline Sturgis—all intimate with Margaret Fuller. Margaret with her radian genius & fiery heart was perhaps the real centre that drew so many & so various individuals to a seeming union. Hedge, Clarke, W. H. Channing, W. E. Channing, jr., George Ripley, James Clarke & many more then or since known as writers, or otherwise distinguished, were only held together as her friends. Mr. A. Bronson Alcott became known to all these as the pure idealist, not at all a man of letters, nor of any practical talent, & quite too cold & contemplative for the alliances of friendship, but purely intellectual, with rare simplicity & grandeur of perception, who read Plato as an equal, & inspired his companions only in proportion as they were intellectual, whilst the men of talent, of course, complained of the want of point & precision in this abstract & religious thinker. Elizabeth Hoar & Sarah Clarke, though certainly never summoned to any of the meetings which were held at George Ripley's, or Dr Francis's, or Stetson's, or Bartol's or whom I have named, in the circle. The

"Dial" was the only public or quotable result of this temporary society & fermentation: and yet the Community at Brook Farm, founded by the readers of Fourier, drew also inspirations from this circle. . . .

In warmer & more fruitful climate Alcott & his friends would soon have been Buddhists.

Actually, in a warmer and more fruitful climate, none of this would have happened at all. New England Transcendentalism was spawned by a rebellious nonconformity among its most impassioned adherents. Although these hardy New England seekers were decidedly individual in their pursuits, they possessed in common a firm rejection of traditions, be they religious, social, artistic, or educational. In that respect they were annoying to the satisfied and preposterous to the merely complacent. It is no wonder, therefore, that in the next century, figures such as Mahatma Gandhi and Martin Luther King, Jr., found in their tone a vibrant source of inspiration for their own revolutions.

In this section we look more closely at the personal quests of individuals, this because although these people often met in groups and held conversations, they did search privately for their truths and sifted through their inner lives as solitaries. In fact, their occasional gatherings, such as the Transcendental Club, begun by Frederic Hedge, seldom produced much that could be called a common set of beliefs or any agreement whatsoever about the nature of their cause. The best that can be said of their communal efforts, including Brook Farm, is that they shared a common sentiment, which centered on the notion of the infinitude of the private individual and the need to reform the culture of the day.

The Transcendentalists gathered around this central fire. The individuals—Emerson, Hedge, Clarke, Brownson, Fuller, Peabody,

Channing, Alcott, Thoreau, and Ripley—fed the fire with their own logs and kindling and then joined the others at the edge, content to share the warmth of the circle itself but nonetheless alone with their thoughts. As they warmed themselves in mutuality, however, they were also aware of the dark abyss behind them. Theirs was a sojourn in the philosophical wilderness, but nonetheless embarked upon willingly, even enthusiastically. Despite their solitary progress, the sense of comradery was still very important and useful, as it usually is around a shared campfire.

In addition to the solitary nature of their quests, another characteristic of the movement was its birth and generation in the midst of a powerful sense of loss or disillusionment. These individuals commonly experienced a profound dislocation from their ordinary spiritual and intellectual worlds. The traditions in which they were raised and nurtured, whether Unitarian, Calvinist, or the classical curriculum of Harvard itself, failed them, failed to provide the teaching, the textual authority, or the rigor they were seeking. Time and time again, we find in their writing a starting point based on loss or suffering, or at the very least aversion.

Initially, their voluntary separation from tradition left them in doubt and isolation. A typical example of such loss and isolation is portrayed in Jones Very's sonnet "The Dead," in which he characterizes the unthinking passage through life as seen through the eyes of one who looks from outside.

THE DEAD
I see them crowd on crowd they walk the earth
Dry, leafless trees no Autumn wind laid bare;
And in their nakedness find cause for mirth,
And all unclad would winter's rudeness dare:

No sap doth through their clattering branches flow,
Whence springing leaves and blossoms bright appear;
Their hearts the living God have ceased to know,
Who gives the spring time to th'expectant year;
They mimic life, as if from him to steal
His glow of health to paint the livid cheek;
They borrow words for thoughts they cannot feel,
That with a seeming heart their tongue may speak;
And in their show of life more dead they live
Than those that to the earth with many tears they give.

Very (1813–1880), a younger member of the circle, is typical of those who saw themselves in an elite group of "conscious" beings awake to the spiritual life and separate from what they perceived as the ignorant masses. This ego-inflating "excess of awareness" was typical of an early stage of this journey, where the individual feels both different and separate from his former acquaintances and thus in some way superior to them. The older and wiser members of the circle, such as Emerson, Channing, and Hedge, knew better than to indulge in this kind of self-aggrandizing, egotistical exultation.

Nonetheless, Very's criticism of those who in deadly ignorance walk the earth speaks accurately to the example of Plato's cave dwellers, those who persist in living in unthinking acceptance of sensory evidence. These shadow dwellers never question what their senses report and live in ignorance of the light beyond the cave entrance. In stark contrast to "The Dead" is another of Very's sonnets, this one celebrating his own personal experience in being liberated from Plato's cave and discovering the central values of the Transcendental vision.

ON FINDING THE TRUTH

With sweet surprise, as when one finds a flower,
Which in some lonely spot, unheeded grows;
Such were my feelings, in the favored hour,
When Truth to me her beauty did disclose.
Quickened I gazed anew on heaven and earth,
For a new glory beamed from earth and sky;
All things around me shared the second birth,
Restored with me, and nevermore to die.
The happy habitants of other spheres,
As in times past, from heaven and earth came down;
Swift fled in converse sweet the unnumbered years,
And angel-help did human weakness crown!
The former things, with Time, had passed away,
And Man, and Nature lived again for aye.

The theme of second birth echoes Emerson's line from "Fate," in which he employs the biblical notion of being born again in Christ, so familiar in Charismatic circles, but he transforms it into a series of self-reflective experiences in the quest for the truth of reality. Emerson said, "The revelation of Thought takes man out of servitude into freedom. We rightly say of ourselves, we were born, and afterward we were born again, and many times."

The idea of the second birth in consciousness was a critical component of the Transcendental vision. Those such as William E. Channing (1780–1842) who were wedded to the orthodoxy of Christian teachings and yet sympathetic to the new thinking nevertheless could not share the substance of the vision. They did not see themselves as somehow separate, nor did they share the experience of great loss in their quest for faith and truth.

But the *essential* Transcendentalists did know the terrors of doubt and the agonies of separation in their initial experiences with the vast reaches of infinitude. In their writings these seekers were willing to confess to these feelings and to describe in detail the sensations associated with spiritual rebirth. This willingness to throw off the reserve and formalisms of religious and philosophical writing contributed to the assessment among many that these people were more than misfits and heretics, that indeed they were more than likely deranged. Even though the witch trials of Salem were more than a century old, such memories lingered. In fact, Emerson could number among his ancestors not only the infamous Anne Hutchinson but also the judge who condemned her to exile.

The accusation of insanity was not some offhand dismissal of a local crank. Ralph Waldo Emerson came from a Brahmin family, the elite of Boston society, even though the family became impoverished when his father, William, died when Ralph Waldo was only seven. Harvard educated and ordained a Unitarian minister, Emerson had embarked on a traditional career. But when his first wife, Ellen, succumbed to tuberculosis at nineteen, leaving Emerson bereft, he resigned from his post as Junior Minister of the Second Church of Boston, leaving many to think he was throwing his life away and would amount to nothing.

Although grief and loneliness played a role in his resignation from the Church and subsequent decision to embark on the life of an independent scholar, none of these circumstances would have been crucial had it not been for his constitutional need to explore the essential mysteries of the human condition and the secrets of nature. As we learn from his journals, the resignation from the Church was primarily an intellectual one. The decision came from character and only found its particular expression from the circumstances of the life. There was, then, in Emerson and the other Transcendentalists an impulse from character first and foremost to do and be who they were—free, questioning, solitary scholars.

Although it is true that most of the documents of Transcendentalism speak directly to the human need for transcendence in quasi-religious language, they do so with great intelligence and insight. The texts of Transcendentalism seldom stoop to pedantry and are seldom dogmatic. These eloquent practitioners were instigators rather than explainers. They prodded their readers awake rather than bludgeoning them with argument. Their method was revelation, not analysis. They recorded their insights as they received them, which suggests the Romantic notions of "automatic writing," with the important difference, however, that these writers never attributed their work to departed spirits or mystical guides. The emphasis instead was upon careful discrimination of what was clearly their own. Even its most extreme—as in mystical—voice, Bronson Alcott, made no claim of revelation for his insights but rather expressed a simple trust in their authenticity.

THE SOLITARY JOURNEYS

We begin our deeper exploration of the Transcendental circle with the work of Bronson Alcott, whose journals and teaching made the earliest idealistic impressions. I have also chosen to begin with Alcott because he was the only major figure not to have formal roots in the Church. At one point, for example, meetings of the so-called Transcendental Club were attended only by ordained ministers. Only later were the gatherings broadened to include women and non-clerics.

AMOS BRONSON ALCOTT

As we learn from Bliss Perry, whose recently reprinted 1950 anthology *The Transcendentalists* is now one of two comprehensive anthologies in print, Emerson was reading Alcott's journal as early as 1834–35, as he wrote *Nature,* the founding document of the movement. That Alcott was subsequently overshadowed by Emerson was due in part to the brilliance of *Nature* when it appeared in 1836 and in part to Alcott's own inability to find the means to express his vision in a form convivial to readers of the time. Unlike Emerson's journals, Alcott's were too personal to be gleaned for useful material, and as a result his attempts to frame essays ended in disjointed failures.

Alcott may have been the most prolific unpublished writer of his time. For example, Odell Shepard's copious five-hundred-page *Journals of Bronson Alcott* is the only readily accessible record of Alcott's writing, and it represents but one-twentieth of the five million words transcribed over his lifetime. Unlike Emerson's journals and notebooks, which are more the record of a scholar and less a personal diary, Alcott's entries were highly personal, self-reflective and self-effacing, as well as being a complete record of the time. As such, they represent some of the most accurate history of Transcendentalism in our possession. It is unfortunate that they remain in unpublished obscurity.

As we learn from Shepard, and he is certainly correct, Alcott wrote as an exercise in self-awareness, to know himself through the exercise of seeing his thoughts on the page. Reading the entries later, he would come to know himself better, to seek the practical ends of self-improvement, calmness, duty, and responsibility, but also, less practically, to know the deep, undiscovered source of his being. If he was, in the world's eyes, a somewhat bizarre, obscure, and ineffectual citizen, in the journals he was nothing if not sensitive, thoughtful, observant, kind, intelligent, and deeply spiritual. In other words, Alcott was a man well worth knowing.

Alcott's is the story of the Transcendentalists writ small, at least as seen by society at large. Accused of being idle, impractical, and solitary to a fault, these individuals were also the dreamers and diarists of the spirit. Like Jack and his bean stalk, if you sent a Transcendentalist like Alcott off to market to sell the cow, he returned a year later having climbed to heaven and back, with no discernible profit and no cow. But then, given some peace and quiet, he wrote golden narratives of his journey, a greater boon than anything he might have gained in the marketplace.

Alcott's journey of self-discovery began at the age of fifteen when he left his father's flax farm in Wolcott, Connecticut, to earn his own way in the world as a peddler in Southern states. Schooled informally by his mother and inspired by John Bunyan's *Pilgrim's Progress,* Amos Bronson was always alert to the inner life, and although he returned home without having been a success in sales, he had learned that he had a great gift in conversation and that teaching might be a suitable career.

As he explored the methods of education available at the time, it was the system of Swiss educator Johann Heinrich Pestalozzi (1746–1827) that attracted his interest and attention. In small schools in Connecticut, Pennsylvania, and finally Boston, Alcott perfected the Pestalozzi principles until they became grafted on to his own personality and vision. Because these principles so closely parallel Transcendental ideas and form the basis of educational idealism, they are worth setting down.

The following points are among those articulated by William Kilpatrick in his introduction to Pestalozzi's work:[18]

1. Personality is sacred. This constitutes the inner dignity of each individual for the young as truly as for the adult.
2. As "a little seed . . . contains the design of the tree," so in each child is the promise of his potentiality. The educator only takes care that no untoward influence shall disturb nature's march of developments.
3. Love of those we would educate is "the sole and everlasting foundation" in which to work. "Without love, neither the physical nor the intellectual powers will develop naturally." So kindness ruled in Pestalozzi's schools: he abolished flogging—much to the amazement of outsiders.

Frankly, it was the rare educator then or now who would continue to read beyond the first principle. *Personality is sacred?* Most schoolmasters of the period were busy just keeping "the little monsters" in line and seldom spared the rod rather than providing the love spoken of by Pestalozzi. The traditional aim, in Lockean terms, was to take the *tabula rasa* of the young mind and fill it with the tools and information required to fit the pupil into society to become a useful citizen. The "personality" was, for the most part, merely in the way and had to be brought under discipline. It would be Alcott's vision not only to affirm the uniqueness of each individual but to identify that uniqueness as a sacred vessel, teaching that within each vessel there dwelled a soul to be awakened and nurtured.

By the time Alcott reached Boston and opened the Temple School, he had a clear vision of how young minds could be nurtured. He often reflected in his journals that when he encountered adults, it was too late to awaken them to the examined life, but children were still open and curious. The difficulty inherent in his program is that Alcott, too, had a system he hoped to implant, in this case a spiritual one, and the record of his "conversations with children" revealed a clear effort to influence them along particular lines of thought, and it was probably this, more than any specific method of instruction that doomed the school to failure.

This said, however, the record of the Temple School experiment remains an inspiration to many educators, and even in Alcott's own time his influence spread out from New England to the west and even to Great Britain, where similar schools were founded following Alcott's and Pestalozzi's principles.

More broadly, Alcott's life and influence were unabashedly metaphysical. He dwelled in the depths of being and provided, particularly in conversation, a consistent example of living in the spirit. The following passage from the journals of 1835, though not typical of his prose, expresses the complexity of his vision.

I set out from the wide ground of spirit. This is; all else is its manifestation. Body is Spirit at its circumference. It denotes its confines to the external sense; it individualizes, defines Spirit, breaks the Unity into Multiplicity and places under the vision of man parts of the great Whole which, standing thus separate, can be taken in by the mind—too feeble to apprehend the whole at once and requiring all save an individual thing to be excluded at a single view. Infinitude is too wide for man to take in. He is therefore permitted to take in portions and spread his vision over the wide circumference by little and little; and in these portions doth the Infinite shadow forth itself, God in all and all in God.

It would take the eloquence of Emerson in particular to put flesh on this spirit, and over the next thirty years Alcott would see his vision expanded upon and made practical in Emerson's works. The debt is clear enough, even if the words are strictly Emerson's. Infinitude is the theme to be expanded upon. Emerson used the image of the circle to express it. He said that his essays, his brief explorations into the nature of the infinite, were each small arcs in that great circle, which never closed but rather spiraled out and up in the effort to envision the wide circumference.

RALPH WALDO EMERSON (1803–1882)

On July 15, 1838, Ralph Waldo Emerson addressed the half dozen graduates of Divinity College at Harvard. He had been invited by the graduates, who had been impressed some months before by an informal session with him in Cambridge. Emerson knew that this opportunity to give a formal address at Divinity College, of which he himself was a graduate, would be his chance to influence the future direction of the Unitarian worship in New England.

So offensive to authority was this address that Emerson would not be invited back to speak at Harvard for more than thirty years. The entrenched attitudes among the faculty of Divinity College were so deeply embedded that what we now see as mild criticism was received by the faculty as nothing less than heresy. The greatest offense was his reference to Jesus as a man and not God incarnate, which for most Christians was and remains heretical, but Emerson's point was to affirm the human being as infinite as well. Here is the relevant passage:

And now, my brothers, you will ask, What in these desponding days can be done by us? The remedy is already declared in the ground of our complaint of the Church. We have contrasted the Church with the Soul. In the soul, then, let the redemption be sought. Wherever a man comes, there comes revolution. The old is for slaves. When a man comes, all books are legible, all things transparent, all religions are forms. He is religious. Man is the wonderworker. He is seen amid miracles. All men bless and curse. He saith yea and nay, only. The stationariness of religion; the assumption that the age of inspiration is past, that the Bible is closed; the fear of degrading the character of Jesus by representing him as a man; indicate with sufficient clearness the falsehood of our theology. It is the office of a true teacher to show us that God is, not was; that He speaketh, not spake. The true Christianity,—a faith like Christ's in the infinitude of man,—is lost. None believeth in the soul of man, but only in some man or person old and departed.

Understood in the context of Locke and Hume and against the empirical tendencies influencing the Unitarian Church at the time, Emerson's plea to reinstate the human capacity for a personal, authentic spiritual life should have been received as an effort at balance, but the theologians present heard only the criticism of their Church and the doctrines it supported. The evidence of their reactions to Emerson's sermon reveals that they hardly understood the extent to which they had already succumbed to the theological revisionism of the times.

Emerson waved off the controversy set off by his address, calling it a storm in a teacup, but privately he was surprised by the severity of the reaction from his fellow divines. The young graduates, on the other hand, were delighted by the message and urged Emerson to publish the address, which he did. The result was that he was forever relieved of the temptation to return to the Church

or to serve as a guest minister, which, up to that time, he had
been doing.

To give a sense of Emerson's spiritual development in this pivotal period, it would be instructive to juxtapose his published
thought in *Nature* with his public remarks at Divinity College
two years later. The differences may in part relate to a journal
entry in May 1837, a long, impassioned entry, small segments of
which appeared in later essays, but never the entire passage. His
revelatory outburst made his spiritual position abundantly clear,
and it was surely something he shared privately with Alcott and
Fuller, to name two of his closest friends.

JOURNAL C, MAY 26, 1837

*Who shall define to me an Individual? I behold with awe
& delight many illustrations of the One universal Mind. I see
my being imbedded in it. As a plant in the earth so I grow in
God. I am only a form of him. He is the soul of me. I can even
with a mountainous aspiring say, I am God, by transferring my
Me out of the flimsy & unclean precincts of my body, my fortunes, my private will, & meekly retiring upon the holy aus-
terities of the Just & the Loving—upon the secret fountains of
Nature. That thin & difficult ether, I also can breathe. The
mortal lungs & nostrils burst & shrivel, but the soul itself
needeth no organs, it is all element & all organ. Yet why not
always so? How came the Individual thus armed & impassioned to parricide, thus murderously inclined ever to traverse
& kill the divine life. Ah wicked Manichee! Into that dim
problem I cannot enter. A believer in Unity, a seer of Unity, I
yet behold two. Whilst I feel myself in sympathy with Nature
& rejoice with greatly beating heart in the course of Justice &
Benevolence overpowering me, I yet find little access to this Me*

of Me. I fear what shall befal; I am not enough a party to the Great Order to be tranquil. I hope & I fear. I do not see. At one time, I am a Doer. A divine life, I create scenes & persons around & for me & unfold my thought by a perpetual successive projection. At least I so say, I so feel. But presently I return to the habitual attitude of suffering. I behold; I bask in beauty; I await; I wonder; Where is my Godhead now? This is the Male & Female principle in nature. One man, male & female created he him. Hard as it is to describe God, it is harder to describe the Individual. A certain wandering light comes to me which I instantly perceive to be the Cause of Causes. It transcends all proving. It is itself the ground of being; and I see that it is not one & I another, but this is the life of my life. That is one fact then; that in certain moments I have known that I existed directly from God, and am, as it were, his organ. And in my ultimate consciousness Am He.

Here in one outpouring is Emerson's infinitude of the private man. What can infinitude mean if not unity with the ground of being, and what can unity mean if not identity with it? And yet how can a human being, enlightened or not, claim identity with the Universal Mind, or the mind of God? Emerson asserts "I Am He" in the same sense that the Hindu says *Tat Twam Asi,* or "Thou art That," in exactly the same sense. The only way in which unity can ever be expressed is through identity with the source. The concept is accepted in the East. For the Manichaean West, however, unity is still a foreign concept.

When Emerson says, realistically, "yet I behold two," he affirms that in our ordinary sense-based experience, duality is the operative condition. We are located firmly in a world of polarities, and yet to stop there, to believe that this fragmented view of reality is all we have, ignores the hidden sources of creation and meaning in existence. All is One, Emerson says, and here is the fundamental Transcendental vision. All the rest is details.

In "The Transcendentalist," Emerson makes a comprehensive distinction between the two points of view of reality. It might first be useful to point out that, as the old joke has it, there are two kinds of people in the world: those who divide things into twos and those who don't. In Emerson's case, he simplifies the dualistic state of worldviews by stating that the world is ever divided into two parties: the materialists and the idealists. This oversimplification is a practical way of addressing his subject, but is not meant to reflect the reality in society. For one thing, materialists make up the vast majority of people, whereas the idealists generally struggle in solitude and hardly know one another.

The complexity of the tension between the two sects derives from the following set of perceptions, as Emerson expressed the problem in the essay:

> It is well known to most of my audience, that the Idealism of the present day acquired the name of Transcendental, from the use of that term by Immanuel Kant, of Konigsberg, who replied to the skeptical philosophy of Locke, which insisted that there was nothing in the intellect which was not previously in the experience of the senses, by showing that there was a very important class of ideas, or imperative forms, which did not come by experience, but through which experience was acquired; that these were intuitions of the mind itself; and he denominated them "Transcendental" forms.

The Kantian phrase "through which the experience was acquired" takes us into the realm of idealism. The class of facts by which unity is known comes not from experience itself but through the faculties of mind that interpret experience. The philosopher Eric Voegelin (1901–1985) began a study of the search for the ground of being by saying, "Reality is not an object of consciousness but the something in which consciousness occurs as an event of participation between partners in the community of being."[19] Where we place reality in the context of our thinking lives is crucial to the outcome of our explorations. If, as Voegelin asserts, reality is the something within which consciousness occurs and is not in itself the object of our search, then we can trust that we are, as he puts it, truly partners in the community of being. Certainly Emerson thought that was the case.

The next question raised by Emerson in the above passage from "The Transcendentalist" relates to the phrase "imperative forms," taken from Kant. It was Kant's assertion that human beings possessed an inherent faculty called "reason," which because it had an inherent structure related to reality itself, equipped us to achieve an understanding of the nature of things. In other words, we are hardwired by nature to penetrate into the core of things. This set of "imperative," or commanding, forms in the mind became for Emerson the basis for his notion of instinct.

Instinct for Emerson was the formative faculty of the inner life. Although he began to use the term cautiously, he eventually used the term more than one hundred times in his published works, all referring to its perceptive powers and urging his readers to trust its lights. In *Nature,* for example, the term does not appear until the end, and even then it is couched in the sublime utterings of the "Orphic Poet," who sings of the elemental human being as one who "perceives that if his law is still paramount, if still he have elemental power, if his word is sterling yet in nature, it is not conscious power, it is not inferior but superior to his will. It is Instinct."

The very next year, 1837, in "The American Scholar," his Phi Beta Kappa address before the students and faculty of Harvard College, the word "instinct" appears immediately in reference to a sign of the mind's fundamental thirst for knowledge, but soon the word takes on a greater significance. Instinct becomes the mind's ability to find unity amid the appearances of duality; in other words, the mind possesses a unifying instinct.

As the speech unfolds, Emerson boldly states his transcendental theme, and "instinct" is a central term in it.

> The world,—this shadow of the soul, or other me, lies wide around. Its attractions are the keys which unlock my thoughts and make me acquainted with myself. I run eagerly into this resounding tumult. I grasp the hands of those next to me, and take my place in the ring to suffer and to work, taught by an instinct, that so shall the dumb abyss be vocal with speech. I pierce its order; I dissipate its fear; I dispose of it within the circuit of my expanding life.

The idea of an intuitive grasp or instinctive knowledge of the true nature of things became for Emerson and the other Transcendentalists more than a mere hunch or feeling of essential truths. It was fundamental to their understanding of themselves and the world. A growing trust in intuition gave them the confidence to assert their beliefs in the face of the sense-based experience of the materialists, many of whom sat in the audience that day in Cambridge.

Emerson's affirmation of self-trust through instinct gained currency throughout the next twenty years, supported as it was by Kant's cogent arguments, and it was not really until Darwin's *The Origin of Species* in 1859 and then, much later, Freud's "discovery" of the unconscious that the simple use of the word *instinct* and its cousin *intuition* became troublesome. After Darwin, instinct generally meant hereditary habit applied to lower forms of life. After 1860, then, instinct meant species-specific programming, and the word could not be used to describe a mental faculty related to intuitive knowing.

But prior to this cultural shift in meanings, the words as employed by the Transcendentalists described a unique sense of the mind's grasp of reality. For Emerson, instinct was an animating force and a principle of human nature. He knew, of course, that a baby displayed a genetic sucking instinct from the moment of birth, but that primitive instinct was only the crudest expression of the principle in the human being. Instinct was also a faculty of the intellect at the highest level, as we see in this passage from "The Transcendentalist":

> I mean, we have yet no man who has leaned entirely on his character, and eaten angels' food; who, trusting to his sentiments, found life made of miracles; who, working for universal aims, found himself fed, he knew not how; clothed, sheltered, and weaponed, he knew not how, and yet it was done by his own hands. Only in the instinct of the lower animals, we find the suggestion of the methods of it, and something higher than our understanding.

Most famously, Emerson also used "instinct" to affirm just how important the faculty was to establish a firm place to stand, describing that place as the core of self-reliance, by saying in "The

American Scholar," "If the single man plant himself indomitably on his instincts, and there abide, the huge world will come round to him."

So, too, the word *intuition* became the means by which these foundational instincts could be found. Today, we think of intuition as a feeling, a hunch that something is either right or wrong. Rather than unthinkingly following someone else's direction or insight, we intuit our own sense of the situation by an act of inner listening or sensing. But for Emerson, intuition also had a deeper foundation. Following the definitions of the word from Scholastic philosophy, Emerson meant by it a spiritual perception, an immediate knowledge of reality arising from spiritual sources. Even in modern philosophy, the word *intuition* implies an immediate apprehension unsifted, or for that matter, uncensored, by any reasoning process.

These definitions characterized the thought and vision of all the Transcendentalists in some degree. But as much as they affirmed enthusiastically both instinct and intuition as instruments of perception, they were much more circumspect about so-called mystical experiences, at least in part because their detractors watched carefully for any sign of "insanity" in their writings and in part because spiritual excesses were rampant throughout New England and even more so farther west. After all, America was the land of religious freedom and that literally meant the freedom to believe anything, experience everything, and to claim in the name of revelation insights of all kinds.

As noted in "Primary Sources," Emerson included the "transparent eye-ball" experience in *Nature* in order to connect spiritual perception with the absence of ego, which for any reasoning person is crucial. If a hint of the Universal Mind or some aspect of God is to be perceived, "all mean egotism vanishes," as Emerson reported. It would be natural enough, he knew, for the ego to exalt itself as the perceiving faculty, resulting at the very least in a feeling of superiority and at worst a messiah complex.

In another instance, recorded only in his journal, Emerson described another such moment on the afternoon of April 10, 1834, as he was visiting Mount Auburn Cemetery. Here again, he notes the transparency of his perception, an unimpeded glimpse into the secrets of nature.

> *I forsook the tombs & found a sunny hollow where the east wind could not blow & lay down against the side of a tree to most happy beholdings. At least I opened my eyes & let what would pass through them into my soul. I saw no more my relation how near & petty to Cambridge or Boston, I heeded no more what minute or hour our Massachusetts clocks might indicate—I saw only the noble earth on which I was born, with the great Star which warms & enlightens it. I saw the clouds that hang their significant drapery over us,—It was Day, that was all Heaven said.[20]*

These moments of opening out into Nature were not a commonplace in Emerson's life. Indeed, two days later he recalled a couplet from Wordsworth reflecting the rarity of these experiences.

> *'Tis the most difficult of tasks to keep*
> *Heights which the soul is competent to gain.[21]*

Rare though these experiences were, they sustained Emerson as an integrating power in his daily life, informing his writing and maintaining his essential optimism in the face of life's darker times, hence the comment at the outset about forsaking the tombs. The essential image in both these experiences is the relation of the transparent eye to the soul and the direct communication with light as the medium. The later addition of Wordsworth's prosaic comment affirms the capacity of the soul to receive this light, beyond which it is up to the individual's poetic gifts to translate the experience into a confirmation of instinct.

The Mount Auburn experience came soon after his return from Europe, where he had gone to escape the two decisive experiences of his young life: the death of his first wife, Ellen, at age nineteen and his resignation from the Church the following year. His deep love for Ellen was not matched by devotion to his chosen profession, which he had fallen into out of duty and heredity. He was not suited by character to institutional loyalty or to the common duties of the ministry. The question in 1834, lurking in the background of his cemetery visit, then became, "What am I to do?"

His early journals reveal a clear ambition to achieve prominence through eloquence, a gift he recognized in himself from the beginning. He was not, he knew, an exacting scholar, preferring to read for inspiration rather than for systematic study. Tending to glean rather than analyze, he was quick to grasp the essentials of other writers and then to find just the phrase to make those essentials vivid. As the essays and lectures testify to so clearly, his style was aphoristic, making the essays difficult to characterize by topic or sustained argument. As "Circles" intimates, his style and vision resembles the effect of a stone dropped in water, a rippling out of waves of thought, beginning with *Nature* in 1836.

The two essays by Emerson selected for this volume have at their core a concern for the theme of infinitude. In "The Transcendentalist," he set aside, at least at the outset, his habitual aphoristic style and offered a more linear explanation of the movement to which Emerson and his friends had been attached since the publishing of *Nature* six years earlier. The essay begins with the effort to break down the walls imposed by his critics. Emerson would not be pigeonholed or confined to a system or a narrow movement, philosophic or aesthetic. His instinct was always to open out, expand the realms of human experience, both because he was not a narrow thinker himself and because he believed that the universe as revealed in natural law would reveal all that the human mind wished to know if only the individual could remain fully open to its intuitively revealed truths.

Emerson begins with an allusion to light, an echo of the Mount Auburn experience from his 1834 journal. By way of introducing his idealistic theme, he employs the phenomenon of light in a way that prefigures the revolution in physics begun by James Clerk Maxwell in 1878 and expanded on by Albert Einstein in 1905. Emerson said, "The light is always identical in its composition, but it falls on a great variety of objects, and by so falling is first revealed to us, not in its own form, for it is formless, but in theirs; in like manner, thought only appears in the objects it classifies."

Emerson digs into his subject, first, with a quick generalization: "As thinkers, mankind have ever divided into two sects, Materialists and Idealists; the first class founding on experience, the second on consciousness." He makes this fundamental comment in order to drive home a subsequent point. A materialist, he observes, can elevate his understanding of the world to the higher level of idealism, but the idealist will never become a materialist. Affirming that the world does indeed exist, the idealist, Emerson argues, "in speaking of events, sees them as spirits. He does not deny the sensuous fact: by no means." Rather, he sees beyond, through, into a transparency of nature where its laws are to be revealed.

We are much more comfortable now with this notion, especially since the world of quantum mechanics has complicated our grasp of natural law. The New Physics has revealed secrets so complex and baffling that no thinking person can readily deny that ordinary experience has an illusory quality and that the truth of reality does not yield itself to commonsense thinking. What we eventually make of these baffling facts will define how we understand the universe. As Einstein said, "Everything has changed except our way of thinking." Despite our sophisticated knowledge, mystery remains at the core of our experience.

Emerson's point is that our way of thinking will naturally encompass idealism, as he defines it, because we are born to it, and if our thought fails to imagine the depths surrounding us, we are confined to ordinary (read ignorant) existence. The either-or nature of his approach may strike us as severe, but the resulting shock to the system is what is necessary to crack open our perception. As Emerson points out, the materialist is so certain of his sense-based view of things that only this kind of severity will do, in order to shake loose the arrogant certainty of the position.

One of Emerson's dominant themes is the difference between the conscious life of the mind and its opposite: repose. In "Intellect" he puts the matter as another of life's polarities:

> God offers to every mind its choice between truth and repose. Take which you please,—you can never have both. Between these, as a pendulum, man oscillates. He in whom the love of repose predominates will accept the first creed, the first philosophy, the first political party he meets,— most likely his father's. He gets rest, commodity, and reputation; but he shuts the door of truth. He in whom the love of truth predominates will keep himself aloof from all moorings, and afloat. He will abstain from dogmatism, and recognize all the opposite negations, between which, as walls,

his being is swung. He submits to the inconvenience of suspense and imperfect opinion, but he is a candidate for truth, as the other is not, and respects the highest law of his being.

This polarity echoes the Jones Very poem (see page 64) in which the dead walk the streets oblivious of their surroundings and their potential infinitude. What is also clear is that the choice is not about morality and immorality—in other words, not about behavior. The choice is about living consciously or not. It is in this choice that human beings experience the release from the bonds of fate into the realms of freedom.

It is then the mission of "The Transcendentalist" to present the practical challenges of the examined life. The path to the truth of reality isn't easy, and Emerson is very clear about its difficulties. He refers elsewhere ("The Over-Soul") to the presence of mere moments of spiritual insight, whereas our vice, as he puts it, is habitual. For a philosopher committed to unity, Emerson seems to spend most of his time dealing with life's polarities. We learn, however, that in order for life to exist at all, polarities are required. The tension of opposites keeps us alive and the universe moving, whereas unity is the nature of the whole, the ground state.

Essays such as "Compensation," "Experience," and "Fate" deal almost exclusively with life lived in duality, but the person who chooses unity possesses the detachment to watch the procession of opposites, the "Lords of Life," as Emerson calls them, pass by. The power to remain detached, to live in unity and experience those rare transparent moments, is the substance of "The Transcendentalist." Emerson defends this detachment from the accusation of the movement's critics, who saw in withdrawal from active life a denial of responsibility. Emerson is unapologetic in asserting that society needs the scholar as much as it needs the laborer. It's a question of talent and calling. The question he poses at the end is less a pleading than a demand of his culture: "Will you not tolerate one or two solitary voices in the land, speaking for thoughts and principles not marketable or perishable?"

As much as "The Transcendentalist" is explanation, it is "Circles" that throws aside argument for inspiration. "Circles" moves from polarity to unity at the very outset and as a result is the most absolute of the essays. In fact, nowhere in the complete works is there an essay quite like it. Its form is clearest, its theme most coherent. Laurence Buell says about "Circles," "Here Emerson most dramatically unmasks himself."[22] By "unmasks" Buell shows us Emerson throwing off his reserve and exposing his true rebellious colors. Here is the reformer in all his intensity, although somewhat disguised by his characteristic kindness and devotion to unity.

If we are forced to pick a year in Emerson's life when his creative, intellectual, and spiritual powers were the most robust and his confidence in his vision most open, it would be 1840. Behind him are *Nature,* "The American Scholar," and the "Divinity School Address," and yet to temper his vision was the death of his son Waldo in 1842 and his changing focus from the ideal to the actual. "Circles" was finished in 1840 and represents, as much as any piece of writing, Emerson's credo: "I unsettle all things. No facts are to me sacred; none are profane; I simply experiment, an endless seeker, with no Past at my back."

What constitutes real life for the seeker? Emerson says, "There is no sleep, no pause, no preservation, but all things renew, germinate, and spring." Everything else is old age: "fever, intemperance, insanity, stupidity, and crime." Instead, he asserts, "let them be lovers; let them behold truth; and their eyes are uplifted, their wrinkles smoothed, they are perfumed again with hope and power."

If we ask how we are to identify this state, this real life, Emerson concludes the essay with sound advice. "The one thing which we seek with insatiable desire is to forget ourselves, to be surprised out of our propriety, to lose our sempiternal memory, and to do something without knowing how or why; in short, to draw a new circle." The notion of forgetting the narrow self is a key element in the lives of all the Transcendentalists. They shared in common the desire to eradicate the cult of personality that might so easily have clung to these radicals.

It is the ego that betrays us in the journey, when the exalted seeker becomes the self-sanctified guru and founds a church of which he or she is the central focus. Transcendentalism was notable for its absence of cult status, its freedom from institutional rigidity. Its solitary culture, in other words, was not so much the result of a determination to live monastically, but was rather a principle observed in most spiritual work. It was Emerson's principle of transparency carefully observed.

It would be too simple to link Transcendentalism to Emerson's chronology, and in fact, the hills and valleys of his own journey fit only partially, as we see in the biography of his close friend Margaret Fuller, whose career peaked at a later date and came to an end too abruptly in tragedy.

MARGARET FULLER (1810–1850)

On July 18, 1850, Margaret Fuller was aboard the American brig *Elizabeth* with her two-year-old-son, Nino, and his father, Count

Ossoli, approaching New York harbor when an early-season hurricane swept the ship past the harbor and slammed it against a sandbar just off Fire Island. By the next morning, July 19, the ship had been smashed to pieces by wind-driven waves, and Margaret, her son, and her husband—along with most of the passengers—perished, drowning, as Emerson wrote in his journal, "within sight of & not more than 60 rods from the shore."[23]

Fuller was forty years old when she died, and until 1843 she had been an integral part of the Transcendentalist circle, especially as editor of *The Dial*, to which she was also a regular contributor. Beginning in 1839, having met Emerson and most of the major Transcendentalists, she began a series of "conversations" in Boston, attended by women eager for more intellectual stimulation than Boston then afforded. Among the women in attendance were Emerson's wife, Lidian, and Sarah Ripley, Elizabeth Hoar, Lydia Parker, and Sophia Peabody—in other words, most of the women associated with the "new thinking" in New England.

Margaret was doubly gifted. She possessed a comprehensive knowledge of German philosophy and English Romantic literature, and she could keep a flow of conversation going in fruitful directions. In addition, as attested by her published work, her mind tended toward the perception of three levels or stages of human development and attainment. She perceived the existence of an ascending consciousness of those who were active seekers. Among the more intellectual, these stages were reflected in approaches to literature, and she wrote about criticism with such stages in mind. In society, she saw the same pattern in the institution of marriage, as men and women came together and developed through intimacy and domestic life.

The two samples of her work in this volume illustrate these stages in the growth of consciousness. The first piece, "A Short

Essay on Critics," was written in 1840, the same year that Emerson wrote "Circles," and it describes the subjective, apprehensive, and comprehensive methods that most critics take in approaching literature. The second excerpt, from "The Great Lawsuit. Man versus Men. Woman versus Women," was written in 1843 and was later expanded and published as *Women in the Nineteenth Century,* generally regarded as the first major feminist work in American literature.

The tendency to focus on stages of consciousness in matters intellectual and social may have arisen from the natural order of Fuller's mind and been strengthened from her time with Emerson, with whom she stayed for three weeks in 1836 when he was completing *Nature,* the structure of which also reflected stages of the human awareness of nature. It was, either way, a strong tendency of the Transcendentalists to see such stages as reflecting how and why people saw the world as either material or spiritual based on their level of intellectual and spiritual attainment.

Fuller's further point in viewing the role of the critic and the roles of men and women in marriage was to illustrate the way in which spiritual maturity manifests itself in judgments about art and qualities of daily life. The subtle, mature critic, Fuller states, sifts work rather than stamps it as good or bad. The mature critic tells the reader what he or she discovered in the work, just as the seeker after truth sifts through the surfaces of things to uncover hidden laws. Being a strong reader is a monumental task and takes great intelligence, but also sympathy and insight. These are qualities Fuller did not see in the journals of her day, where the purpose of criticism seemed to be the opportunity to display one's wit at the expense of the writer in question.

On the more serious matter of the nature of marriage, Fuller was even more radical in her views, at least for her time. Once again seeing the number three as the operative design, Fuller builds through images of marriage her vision of a perfect unity. She begins with the marriage of the common sort, one of convenience, surface, and domestic practicality. The man provides, the woman maintains, and the union thrives, if not in mutual growth and development, at least in matter. This lowest level is the utilitarian.

The second level, and one of great interest to reformers and Fuller herself, was intellectual union. Her examples, from the Rolands of the French Revolution, to William Godwin and Mary Wollstonecraft, to William and Mary Howitt, form the more elevated union of two minds of equal attainment working in concert, supporting each other, if not in common cause, at least in mutual respect, a true meeting of minds on the plane of marriage.

The third and most elevated union possible between man and woman is the spiritual marriage. This third state, Fuller argues, is attained not by educating women to be companions of men but by women arriving at a state of freedom to find their own expression for their own ends, and then, if marriage is chosen, finding in it an even higher form of achievement through the dynamics of the union itself. "Marriage is the natural means of creating a sphere," she says, "of taking root in the earth."

And yet, Fuller was no dreamer, no sentimentalist in matters of love and marriage. She saw the failures and fallacies around her and in her reading. Her grasp of the realities is borne out by the state of the institution in our own era and the understanding that marriage is the most difficult of the spiritual disciplines, undertaken in its highest sense not without an abiding awareness of its challenges.

It is not surprising that a woman of Margaret's intellect and ambition would become almost fixated on the institution of marriage as the focus of her expression. In her weekly conversations and social travels in Boston and New York, and later in Italy, it would be the relations between men and women—on the issues of physical control, emotional power, and financial realities of marriage—that occupied the time. She observed beautiful, brilliant women in marriages both good and bad, and she saw herself as both superior and inferior at once, so that it was through her attitude toward marriage that she worked out her own spiritual destiny.

To this day, for example, it is unclear whether she was in fact legally married to Count Ossoli,[24] and as the fateful ship neared New York in July 1850 with her planning to visit Boston and Concord, whether or not Emerson was concerned about how she would be received. Knowing Margaret, one supposes her arrival would have been a triumph of transcendence.

As the reader will surely see in the following pieces, Fuller had a keen eye for hypocrisy and exhibited a firm determination to speak against the condition of women in America, which she viewed as close to slavery. After her untimely death, Emerson said of her, "To the last her country proves inhospitable to her; brave, eloquent, subtle, accomplished, devoted, constant soul."[25] Indeed, each word was carefully chosen and reflected her urgent intellectual and spiritual concerns.

Of all the social and political issues facing the world today, certainly two are the state of marriage as an institution, with the related role of women in culture, and the environment, with the corresponding relation of human beings to the present and future health of the planet. Fuller's surprisingly relevant concerns with the former and Thoreau's with the latter should confirm the vital presence of these materials to our own journey in the twenty-first century.

HENRY DAVID THOREAU (1817–1862)

On October 22, 1837, a twenty-year-old Henry Thoreau began keeping his journal. Its first entry marks the moment when Emerson asked him, "What are you doing now? Do you keep a journal?"[26] The following entry, really the first of substance, was confessional in nature, on the subject of solitude. "To be alone I find it necessary to escape the present—I avoid myself." It is a young man's anxiety of identity. Recently a graduate of Harvard, he was already questioning the value of that experience and wondering what he should do with the life he had been given.

By the following year, on August 10, 1938, he had the following to say about self-consciousness:

> *If with closed ears and eyes I consult consciousness for a moment, immediately are all walls and barriers dissipated, earth rolls from under me, and I float, by the impetus derived from the earth and the system, a subjective, heavily laden thought, in the midst of an unknown and infinite sea, or else heave and swell like a vast ocean of thought, without rock or headland, where all riddles solved, all straight lines making there their two ends meet, eternity and space gambolling familiarly through my depths. I am from the beginning, knowing no end, no aim. No sun illumines me, for I dissolve all lesser lights in my own intenser and steadier light. I am a restful kernel in the imagination of the universe.*[27]

We recognize, even in the awkwardness and excesses of this writing, the Transcendental themes of the mind's infinitude and the release experienced in those initial "gambolling" moments of inner reflection. Emerson's pointed question ("What are you doing now?") became the instigation of his inner life. As he wrote following that question, "My desire is to know *what* I have lived, that I may know *how* to live henceforth."[28] Within a decade, by 1845, Henry would begin his Walden experiment as a means of answering those questions.

Thoreau's *Walden* has come to be for many the sacred text of Transcendentalism. At least part of the reason for its exalted position, in addition to the text itself, are the two years, two months, and two days Thoreau spent in his cabin, symbolically, if not actually, removed from society. It is certainly the Walden Pond experience and subsequent text that has given Transcendentalism its monastic air and environmental complexion.[29] But in addition, the text itself is the clearest and most dramatic call for personal freedom, individualism, and the examined life that America has yet produced.[30] Its inner journeying stands in stark contrast to the adventurous, "on the road" experimentation of the American frontier experience.

Typical of Henry Thoreau's mature attitude about how to live freely is this journal entry from 1841, when he was twenty-four: "I must not lose any of my freedom by being a farmer and landowner. Most men who enter on any profession are doomed men."[31] Extreme as this position was, it was also an accurate observation of the price we pay for attachments to the land, to institutions, and to other individuals.

In "Fate," Emerson said, " Every spirit makes its house; but afterwards the house confines the spirit." True enough, but it was Thoreau's intention to thwart fate as much as he could. The sojourn at Walden, on a borrowed piece of Emerson's land, was tempting fate, to be sure, but once his reflective experiment was completed, Henry moved on, letting go of the attachment and taking up new duties and projects. The writing of *Walden* occupied him from 1845, when he took up residence in his cabin, until 1854, when the book was published.

From beginning to end of *Walden,* Thoreau seldom makes an observation without its being consciously conceived to further his argument. Every fact is sifted through the tools of self-reflective observation, but even as the observing "I" takes the center stage (a radical point of view for the time), Thoreau's ultimate aim is to let go of the intrusive ego. In December 1841 he writes in his journal, "I want to go soon and live away by the pond, where I shall hear only the wind whispering among the reeds, It will be a success if I have left myself behind."

As to the theme of independence, it was his good friend Ellery Channing who, in March 1845, offered Henry this advice: "I see nothing for you . . . but that field I once christened 'Briars'; go . . . build yourself a hut, and there begin the grand process of devouring yourself alive. I see no alternative, no other hope for you. Eat yourself up." This theme of letting go of the fragmented self with the assistance of nature would become the spiritual task of Henry's exercise and the overriding theme of *Walden.* As Alfred Kazin put it, "Thoreau's best writing is an attempt to get up to the point where he can reduce human experience to communion with nature and this communion to images of total human ecstasy."[32]

I take Kazin to mean that Thoreau's ecstatic purpose was to emulate Emerson's similarly ecstatic "transparent eye-ball" experience as an extended conscious experience, making those moments of union with Emerson's "Over-Soul" something more than momentary and rarified. In effect, *Walden* is an exercise in living at one with the cosmos, in finding and dwelling within a unity that is at once physical, intellectual, and spiritual. Read in that way, *Walden* can be an approximation of that unity seen from the detached position of the reader's art. Also, read in that way, it positions the reader to find his or her way into an examined life based on characteristics that Thoreau names at the very outset as simplicity, independence, magnanimity, and trust.

Two excerpts from *Walden* have been included in the present anthology. The first is Chapter 2: "Where I Lived, and What I Lived For," in which Thoreau is the most explicit about his philosophical stance. As always among the Transcendentalists, the examined life is intimately connected to wakefulness and to the infinite. What is different with Thoreau is that what Emerson framed as philosophy, Thoreau intended to live out. *Walden* becomes, then, the document that expresses the fusion of thought and experience into transcendence and presents the thinker and the doer as an integrated whole. How the individual actually applies the principles of the examined life was Thoreau's experiment. The book is his testimony.

The theme of the examined life appears most vividly near the beginning of the chapter:

We must learn to reawaken and keep ourselves awake, not by mechanical aids, but by an infinite expectation of the dawn, which does not forsake us in our soundest sleep. I know of no more encouraging fact than the unquestionable ability of man to elevate his life by a conscious endeavor. It is something to be able to paint a particular picture, or to carve a statue, and so to make a few objects beautiful; but it is far more glorious to carve and paint the very atmosphere and medium through which we look, which morally we can do. To affect the quality of the day, that is the highest of arts. Every man is tasked to make his life, even in its details, worthy of the contemplation of his most elevated and critical hour.

Here is the theme of extending that "most elevated and critical hour" of heightened consciousness into an integrated whole. And the first steps in the process are simplicity and independence. As tempting, and nearly finalized, as it was to buy the Hollowell place and settle down, his luck—and it was fortune more than choice—in escaping from the purchase showed him the benefits of keeping free from attachments of all kinds. So, too, his relationship to marriage and family. His one proposal of marriage, to Ellen Sewell in November 1840, was met with rejection on the part of her family. In a sense, then, freedom from attachment *happened* to Thoreau.

It is interesting, then, to see that Thoreau's isolation from society and subsequent Walden Pond experience came from much deeper, subconscious sources and unavoidable circumstances than any simple conscious decision. At the last minute, a farmer's wife decided against selling the farm, and another family saw something in the young Thoreau they objected to for their daughter's happiness and well-being. But rather than seeing these events as disappointments or failures, Thoreau assimilated them into signs and symbols for his evolving life. What psychologists might call *sublimation* becomes part of a daily process of conscious transformation.

It is in the powers of the dawn, the clarity of the morning wiping away the dark dreaming mind, that produces for Thoreau the answers to the myriad questions that haunt him. Throughout *Walden,* it is morning that is sublime and brings him always back to the present moment and to nature. To reawaken means, then, to come to oneself each morning and to begin each day with a sense of a deeper renewal.

Chapter 5, entitled "Solitude," is Thoreau's ode to Transcendentalism. Its central paragraph describes his experience with self-reflective solitude:

> Any prospect of awakening or coming to life to a dead man makes indifferent all times and places. The place where that may occur is always the same, and indescribably pleasant to all our senses. For the most part we allow only outlying and transient circumstances to make our occasions. They are, in fact, the cause of our distraction. Nearest to all things is that power which fashions their being. Next to us the grandest laws are continually being executed. Next to us is not the workman whom we have hired, with whom we love so well to talk, but the workman whose work we are.

In "Solitude," Thoreau addresses the most common question he received from his neighbors during his Walden experiment: "Aren't you lonely?" That question was posed one way or another not only to Thoreau but in essence to all the Transcendentalists, making it the essential issue in the public's mind. That question is linked to the other essential ingredient: self-reflective study. Emerson said that when a man is asked to study himself, nothing to him seems less interesting. Why? What, we wonder, can be so important within us that can possibly help us be successful in the world? *Walden* is the most comprehensive answer to that question. Solitude is the philosophical condition in which Thoreau's famous "different drummer" can truly be heard.

Next to us is the workman whose work we are, that and the universal laws executing themselves in our presence. The din of society, of commerce, of entertainment is so pervasive that stepping away from them is nearly as impossible as it appears undesirable. Why would we want to do such a thing in the first place? What benefits accrue? How is our life enhanced?

Thoreau's answer to these important questions emerges in *Walden* as the symmetry of observation and the coherence of ordinary experience deeply felt. He went to the pond as an adventure in discovery, vowing to report honestly what he found there. Fortunately for us, who fear to experiment with such extreme solitude, Thoreau met "with a success unexpected in common hours."

In the intervening years, many have followed his example, undertaking similar excursions into their own interior wilderness for the purpose of finding themselves. It is not necessary to enter a monastery or to travel the world in search of sacred mountaintops or caves in order to find what Thoreau found beside an ordinary pond in Massachusetts. A visit to the site of the cabin makes the point clearly enough. It is not the place but the man, the inner life shared through the writer's art. We might feel a bit closer to the man as we look out at the light dancing on the pond or when we turn to place a stone on the cairn in his memory, but the real essence emerges from the pages. And at Sleepy Hollow Cemetery in Concord, on Authors' Ridge, down the slope from Alcott and Emerson, the small tombstone, only ten inches high, is marked, simply, "Henry." He ended his sojourn at Walden Pond with this observation:

I learned this, at least, by my experiment: that if one advances confidently in the direction of his dreams, and endeavors to live the life which he has imagined, he will meet with a success unexpected in common hours. He will put some things behind, will pass an invisible boundary; new, universal, and more liberal laws will begin to establish themselves around and within him; or the old laws be expanded, and interpreted in his favor in a more liberal sense, and he will live with the license of a higher order of beings. In proportion as he simplifies his life, the laws of the universe will appear less complex, and solitude will not be solitude, nor poverty poverty, nor weakness weakness. If you have built castles in the air, your work need not be lost; that is where they should be. Now put the foundations under them.

FROM CONTEMPLATION TO
ACTION IN THE WORLD

In "The Transcendentalist," Emerson said, "We will wait . . . until the universe rises up and calls us to work," when he was asked if and when these solitaries would or could take action in the world, would involve themselves in public affairs. It was, he knew, a fair question. The examined life is all well and good, but isn't our role to assume an active role in the world, to participate? Emerson wrestled with this question throughout a very difficult period in the history of America. Although he was by instinct a scholar, his natural eloquence as a speaker and writer was in great demand in confronting the important issues of the day.

The world, in fact, would do the calling in its own time when conscious action was required. Emerson's plea to act in the world out of one's self was not a selfish call to act *for* oneself. It was a reminder that we should not take action in the world from the influence of the opinions of others. Human beings, he knew, have the capacity to withdraw from the world for a time to a position of solitary reflection and in that silent space to develop a plan of action, and then, and only then, to return and act from a position of self-knowledge and conviction. Although other Transcendentalists were active as social reformers from the beginning of their careers as ministers, most were regarded as being withdrawn from the ordinary social and commercial life of the time, hence Emerson's defense in "The Transcendentalist."

At the time when the Transcendentalists were particularly active, the central political and social issue for the nation was slavery. As David Robinson points out in his book *The Political Emerson,* it was not until the mid-1840s that Emerson began to write essays and lectures in a new tone of public advocacy. His "New England Reformers" and "Emancipation in the British West Indies" marked this change, and by 1850, when the Fugitive Slave Law was passed, which made it illegal for a citizen in the free state to aid an escaped slave, everything changed, and with it came the gradual end of Transcendentalism as a philosophical movement. It was, in fact, overwhelmed by the approaching Civil War, as often it happens that ideas are subsumed by violent circumstances.

By 1849, the town of Concord had become a center for abolitionist speeches in forums such as the Concord Lyceum, and as a sign of the times, Elizabeth Peabody published a speech by Thoreau in her *Aesthetic Papers* under the title "Resistance to Civil Government." The essay was republished in 1863, after Thoreau's death, but was not well-known until the twentieth century when Mahatma Gandhi and Martin Luther King, Jr., found in it the arguments to support their nonviolent protests.

Thoreau's "Civil Disobedience," as the essay is now known, is the most famous political document arising from Transcendentalism. Here is the central argument of the essay, the hinge on which it swings:

> Can there not be a government in which majorities do not virtually decide right and wrong, but conscience?—in which majorities decide only those questions to which the rule of expediency is applicable? Must the citizen ever for a moment, or in the least degree, resign his conscience to the legislator? Why has every man a conscience, then? I think that we should be men first, and subjects afterward.

What is conscience? Is it moral instinct? Is it a highly developed faculty of conscious thought applied to moral questions? In careful consideration of the laws of the mind, these are not easy questions. Plato thought that conscience was a *daimon* or spiritual power with only one message: No! In this sense, then, conscience arises only as a check to action. It is, as commonly defined, the sense of shame we feel when we have acted improperly.

But conscience can also be more consciously derived, what Emerson called an individual's private wisdom. Here is a passage from his essay "Considerations by the Way":

> We like very well to be praised for our action, but our conscience says, "Not unto us." 'Tis little we can do for each other. We accompany the youth with sympathy, and manifold old sayings of the wise, to the gate of the arena, but 'tis certain that not by strength of ours, or of the old sayings, but only on strength of his own, unknown to us or to any, he must stand or fall. That by which a man conquers in any passage, is a profound secret to every other being in the

world, and it is only as he turns his back on us and on all men, and draws on this most private wisdom, that any good can come to him.

We can say on the basis of the evidence that Thoreau's conscience was highly developed, and certainly one reason for that had to be the effect of his sojourn at Walden Pond, with its ample time for reflection in the midst of nature. Certainly the world since has affirmed the strength of that conscience and has absorbed and applied it to causes as notable as apartheid, civil rights, and war.

What finally adheres, however, in reflecting on New England Transcendentalism is Emerson's profound sense of mystery, what he calls the "profound secret" of how each one of us conquers or fails to do so in the passages of our lives. When Emerson was only sixteen, he discovered the ancient dictum of Archimedes, which said, "Give me a place to stand and I will move the Earth." For the Greek sage it was the principle of leverage, but to the young Emerson it was the principle of self-recovery, of what he called the "erect position." He knew that if and when he could find his place to stand, he could apply the gifts of eloquence he had been given and, perhaps, move the earth. Transcendental idealism was that place.

RALPH WALDO EMERSON

Emerson's "The Transcendentalist" is less inspiration than explanation, and is included here to help clarify the themes of the movement so closely associated with him. The essay is blatantly an argument supporting idealism, but it also includes the kind of in-

stigation for which Emerson is justly famous. If someone is tee-
tering between two worldviews, this essay could tip the scale.
"Circles," on the other hand, is pure inspiration, a lyric celebration of the laws of the universe, visionary, harmonic, and whole.
It will, as a result, make no sense at all to a materialist, so expressive is it of the idealist vision.

THE TRANSCENDENTALIST
A lecture read at the Masonic Temple, Boston, January 1842

The first thing we have to say respecting what are called
"new views" here in New England, at the present time, is,
that they are not new, but the very oldest of thoughts cast
into the mold of these new times. The light is always identical in its composition, but it falls on a great variety of objects, and by so falling is first revealed to us, not in its own
form, for it is formless, but in theirs; in like manner, thought
only appears in the objects it classifies. What is popularly
called Transcendentalism among us, is Idealism; Idealism
as it appears in 1842. As thinkers, mankind have ever divided into two sects, Materialists and Idealists; the first class
founding on experience, the second on consciousness; the
first class beginning to think from the data of the senses, the
second class perceive that the senses are not final, and say,
the senses give us representations of things, but what are the
things themselves, they cannot tell. The materialist insists on
facts, on history, on the force of circumstances, and the animal wants of man; the idealist on the power of Thought
and of Will, on inspiration, on miracle, on individual culture. These two modes of thinking are both natural, but

the idealist contends that his way of thinking is in higher nature. He concedes all that the other affirms, admits the impressions of sense, admits their coherency, their use and beauty, and then asks the materialist for his grounds of assurance that things are as his senses represent them. But I, he says, affirm facts not affected by the illusions of sense, facts which are of the same nature as the faculty which reports them, and not liable to doubt; facts which in their first appearance to us assume a native superiority to material facts, degrading these into a language by which the first are to be spoken; facts which it only needs a retirement from the senses to discern. Every materialist will be an idealist; but an idealist can never go backward to be a materialist.

The idealist, in speaking of events, sees them as spirits. He does not deny the sensuous fact: by no means; but he will not see that alone. He does not deny the presence of this table, this chair, and the walls of this room, but he looks at these things as the reverse side of the tapestry, as the *other end,* each being a sequel or completion of a spiritual fact which nearly concerns him. This manner of looking at things, transfers every object in nature from an independent and anomalous position without there, into the consciousness. Even the materialist Condillac, perhaps the most logical expounder of materialism, was constrained to say, "Though we should soar into the heavens, though we should sink into the abyss, we never go out of ourselves; it is always our own thought that we perceive." What more could an idealist say?

The materialist, secure in the certainty of sensation, mocks at fine-spun theories, at star-gazers and dreamers, and believes that his life is solid, that he at least takes nothing for granted, but knows where he stands, and what he does. Yet how easy it is to show him, that he also is a phantom walking and working amid phantoms, and that he need only ask a question or two beyond his daily questions, to find his solid universe growing dim and impalpable before his sense. The sturdy capitalist, no matter how deep and square on blocks of Quincy granite he lays the foundations of his banking-house or Exchange, must set it, at last, not on a cube corresponding to the angles of his structure, but on a mass of unknown materials and solidity, red-hot or white-hot, perhaps at the core, which rounds off to an almost perfect sphericity, and lies floating in soft air, and goes spinning away, dragging bank and banker with it at a rate of thousands of miles the hour, he knows not whither,— a bit of bullet, now glimmering, now darkling through a small cubic space on the edge of an unimaginable pit of emptiness. And this wild balloon, in which his whole venture is embarked, is a just symbol of his whole state and faculty. One thing, at least, he says is certain, and does not give me the headache, that figures do not lie; the multiplication table has been hitherto found unimpeachable truth; and, moreover, if I put a gold eagle in my safe, I find it again tomorrow;— but for these thoughts, I know not whence they are. They change and pass away. But ask him why he believes that an uniform experience will continue uniform, or on what grounds he founds his faith in his figures, and he will perceive that his mental fabric is built up on just as strange and quaking foundations as his proud edifice of stone.

In the order of thought, the materialist takes his departure from the external world, and esteems a man as one product of that. The idealist takes his departure from his consciousness, and reckons the world an appearance. The materialist respects sensible masses, Society, Government, social art, and luxury, every establishment, every mass, whether majority of numbers, or extent of space, or amount of objects, every social action. The idealist has another measure, which is metaphysical, namely, the *rank* which things themselves take in his consciousness; not at all, the size or appearance. Mind is the only reality, of which men and all other natures are better or worse reflectors. Nature, literature, history, are only subjective phenomena. Although in his action overpowered by the laws of action, and so, warmly cooperating with men, even preferring them to himself, yet when he speaks scientifically, or after the order of thought, he is constrained to degrade persons into representatives of truths. He does not respect labor, or the products of labor, namely, property, otherwise than as a manifold symbol, illustrating with wonderful fidelity of details the laws of being; he does not respect government, except as far as it reiterates the law of his mind; nor the church; nor charities; nor arts, for themselves; but hears, as at a vast distance, what they say, as if his consciousness would speak to him through a pantomimic scene. His thought,— that is the Universe. His experience inclines him to behold the procession of facts you call the world, as flowing perpetually outward from an invisible, unsounded centre in himself, centre alike of him and of them, and necessitating him to regard all things as having a subjective or relative existence, relative to that aforesaid Unknown Centre of him.

From this transfer of the world into the consciousness, this beholding of all things in the mind, follow easily his whole ethics. It is simpler to be self-dependent. The height, the deity of man is, to be self-sustained, to need no gift, no foreign force. Society is good when it does not violate me; but best when it is likest to solitude. Everything real is self-existent. Everything divine shares the self-existence of Deity. All that you call the world is the shadow of that substance which you are, the perpetual creation of the powers of thought, of those that are dependent and of those that are independent of your will. Do not cumber yourself with fruitless pains to mend and remedy remote effects; let the soul be erect, and all things will go well. You think me the child of my circumstances: I make my circumstance. Let any thought or motive of mine be different from that they are, the difference will transform my condition and economy. I—this thought which is called I,—is the mould into which the world is poured like melted wax. The mould is invisible, but the world betrays the shape of the mould. You call it the power of circumstance, but it is the power of me. Am I in harmony with myself? my position will seem to you just and commanding. Am I vicious and insane? my fortunes will seem to you obscure and descending. As I am, so shall I associate, and, so shall I act; Caesar's history will paint out Caesar. Jesus acted so, because he thought so. I do not wish to overlook or to gainsay any reality; I say, I make my circumstance: but if you ask me, Whence am I? I feel like other men my relation to that Fact which cannot be spoken, or defined, nor even thought, but which exists, and will exist.

The Transcendentalist adopts the whole connection of spiritual doctrine. He believes in miracle, in the perpetual openness of the human mind to new influx of light and power; he believes in inspiration, and in ecstasy. He wishes that the spiritual principle should be suffered to demonstrate itself to the end, in all possible applications to the state of man, without the admission of anything unspiritual; that is, anything positive, dogmatic, personal. Thus, the spiritual measure of inspiration is the depth of the thought, and never, who said it? And so he resists all attempts to palm other rules and measures on the spirit than its own.

In action, he easily incurs the charge of antinomianism by his avowal that he, who has the Lawgiver, may with safety not only neglect, but even contravene every written commandment. In the play of Othello, the expiring Desdemona absolves her husband of the murder, to her attendant Emilia. Afterwards, when Emilia charges him with the crime, Othello exclaims,

"You heard her say herself it was not I."

Emilia replies,

"The more angel she, and thou the blacker devil."

Of this fine incident, Jacobi, the Transcendental moralist, makes use, with other parallel instances, in his reply to Fichte. Jacobi, refusing all measure of right and wrong except the determinations of the private spirit, remarks that there is no crime but has sometimes been a virtue. "I," he says, "am that atheist, that godless person who, in opposition to an imaginary doctrine of calculation, would lie as the dying Desdemona lied; would lie and deceive, as Pylades when he personated Orestes; would assassinate like Timoleon; would perjure myself like Epaminondas, and John de Witt; I would resolve on suicide like Cato; I would commit sacrilege with David; yea, and pluck ears of corn on the Sabbath, for no other reason than that I was fainting for lack of food. For, I have assurance in myself, that, in pardoning these faults according to the letter, man exerts the sovereign right which the majesty of his being confers on him; he sets the seal of his divine nature to the grace he accords."

In like manner, if there is anything grand and daring in human thought or virtue, any reliance on the vast, the unknown; any presentiment; any extravagance of faith, the spiritualist adopts it as most in nature. The oriental mind has always tended to this largeness. Buddhism is an expression of it. The Buddhist who thanks no man, who says, "do not flatter your benefactors," but who, in his conviction that every good deed can by no possibility escape its reward, will not deceive the benefactor by pretending that he has done more than he should, is a Transcendentalist.

You will see by this sketch that there is no such thing as a Transcendental *party;* that there is no pure Transcendentalist; that we know of none but prophets and heralds of such a philosophy; that all who by strong bias of nature have leaned to the spiritual side in doctrine, have stopped short of their goal. We have had many harbingers and forerunners; but of a purely spiritual life, history has afforded no example. I mean, we have yet no man who has leaned entirely on his character, and eaten angels' food; who, trusting to his sentiments, found life made of miracles; who, working for universal aims, found himself fed, he knew not how; clothed, sheltered, and weaponed, he knew not how, and yet it was done by his own hands. Only in the instinct of the lower animals, we find the suggestion of the methods of it, and something higher than our understanding. The squirrel hoards nuts, and the bee gathers honey, without knowing what they do, and they are thus provided for without self-ishness or disgrace.

Shall we say, then, that Transcendentalism is the Saturnalia or excess of Faith; the presentiment of a faith proper to man in his integrity, excessive only when his imperfect obedience hinders the satisfaction of his wish. Nature is transcendental, exists primarily, necessarily, ever works and advances, yet takes no thought for the morrow. Man owns the dignity of the life which throbs around him in chemistry, and tree, and animal, and in the involuntary functions of his own body; yet he is balked when he tries to fling himself into this enchanted circle, where all is done without degradation. Yet genius and virtue predict in man the same absence of private ends, and of condescension to circumstances, united with every trait and talent of beauty and power.

This way of thinking, falling on Roman times, made Stoic philosophers; falling on despotic times, made patriot Catos and Brutuses; falling on superstitious times, made prophets and apostles; on popish times, made protestants and ascetic monks, preachers of Faith against the preachers of Works; on prelatical times, made Puritans and Quakers; and falling on Unitarian and commercial times, makes the peculiar shades of Idealism which we know.

It is well known to most of my audience, that the Idealism of the present day acquired the name of Transcendental, from the use of that term by Immanuel Kant, of Konigsberg, who replied to the skeptical philosophy of Locke, which insisted that there was nothing in the intellect which was not previously in the experience of the senses, by showing that there was a very important class of ideas, or imperative forms, which did not come by experience, but through which experience was acquired; that these were intuitions of the mind itself; and he denominated them *Transcendental* forms. The extraordinary profoundness and precision of that man's thinking have given vogue to his nomenclature, in Europe and America, to that extent, that whatever belongs to the class of intuitive thought, is popularly called at the present day *Transcendental.*

Although, as we have said, there is no pure Transcendentalist, yet the tendency to respect the intuitions, and to give them, at least in our creed, all authority over our experience, has deeply colored the conversation and poetry of the present day; and the history of genius and of religion in these times, though impure, and as yet not incarnated in any powerful individual, will be the history of this tendency.

It is a sign of our times, conspicuous to the coarsest observer, that many intelligent and religious persons withdraw themselves from the common labors and competitions of the market and the caucus, and betake themselves to a certain solitary and critical way of living, from which no solid fruit has yet appeared to justify their separation. They hold themselves aloof: they feel the disproportion between their faculties and the work offered them, and they prefer to ramble in the country and perish of ennui, to the degradation of such charities and such ambitions as the city can propose to them. They are striking work, and crying out for somewhat worthy to do! What they do, is done only because they are overpowered by the humanities that speak on all sides; and they consent to such labor as is open to them, though to their lofty dream the writing of Iliads or Hamlets, or the building of cities or empires seems drudgery.

Now every one must do after his kind, be he asp or angel, and these must. The question, which a wise man and a student of modern history will ask, is, what that kind is? And truly, as in ecclesiastical history we take so much pains to know what the Gnostics, what the Essenes, what the Manichees, and what the Reformers believed, it would not misbecome us to inquire nearer home, what these companions and contemporaries of ours think and do, at least so far as these thoughts and actions appear to be not accidental and personal, but common to many, and the inevitable flower of the Tree of Time. Our American literature and spiritual history are, we confess, in the optative mood; but whoso knows these seething brains, these admirable radicals, these unsocial worshippers, these talkers who talk the sun and moon away, will believe that this heresy cannot pass away without leaving its mark.

They are lonely; the spirit of their writing and conversation is lonely; they repel influences; they shun general society; they incline to shut themselves in their chamber in the house, to live in the country rather than in the town, and to find their tasks and amusements in solitude. Society, to be sure, does not like this very well; it saith, Whoso goes to walk alone, accuses the whole world; he declareth all to be unfit to be his companions; it is very uncivil, nay, insulting; Society will retaliate. Meantime, this retirement does not proceed from any whim on the part of these separators; but if any one will take pains to talk with them, he will find that this part is chosen both from temperament and from principle; with some unwillingness, too, and as a choice of the less of two evils; for these persons are not by nature melancholy, sour, and unsocial,—they are not stockish or brute,—

but joyous; susceptible, affectionate; they have even more than others a great wish to be loved. Like the young Mozart, they are rather ready to cry ten times a day, "But are you sure you love me?" Nay, if they tell you their whole thought, they will own that love seems to them the last and highest gift of nature; that there are persons whom in their hearts they daily thank for existing,—persons whose faces are perhaps unknown to them, but whose fame and spirit have penetrated their solitude,—and for whose sake they wish to exist. To behold the beauty of another character, which inspires a new interest in our own; to behold the beauty lodged in a human being, with such vivacity of apprehension, that I am instantly forced home to inquire if I am not deformity itself: to behold in another the expression of a love so high that it assures itself,—assures itself also to me against every possible casualty except my unworthiness;—these are degrees on the scale of human happiness, to which they have ascended; and it is a fidelity to this sentiment which has made common association distasteful to them. They wish a just and even fellowship, or none. They cannot gossip with you, and they do not wish, as they are sincere and religious, to gratify any mere curiosity which you may entertain. Like fairies, they do not wish to be spoken of. Love me, they say, but do not ask who is my cousin and my uncle. If you do not need to hear my thought, because you can read it in my face and behavior, then I will tell it you from sunrise to sunset. If you cannot divine it, you would not understand what I say. I will not molest myself for you. I do not wish to be profaned.

And yet, it seems as if this loneliness, and not this love, would prevail in their circumstances, because of the extravagant demand they make on human nature. That, indeed, constitutes a new feature in their portrait, that they are the most exacting and extortionate critics. Their quarrel with every man they meet, is not with his kind, but with his degree. There is not enough of him,—that is the only fault. They prolong their privilege of childhood in this wise, of doing nothing,—but making immense demands on all the gladiators in the lists of action and fame. They make us feel the strange disappointment which overcasts every human youth. So many promising youths, and never a finished man! The profound nature will have a savage rudeness; the delicate one will be shallow, or the victim of sensibility; the richly accomplished will have some capital absurdity; and so every piece has a crack. 'T is strange, but this masterpiece is a result of such an extreme delicacy, that the most unobserved flaw in the boy will neutralize the most aspiring genius, and spoil the work. Talk with a seaman of the hazards to life in his profession, and he will ask you, "Where are the old sailors? do you not see that all are young men?" And we, on this sea of human thought, in like manner inquire, Where are the old idealists? where are they who represented to the last generation that extravagant hope, which a few happy aspirants suggest to ours? In looking at the class of counsel, and power, and wealth, and at the matronage of the land, amidst all the prudence and all the triviality, one asks, Where are they who represented genius, virtue, the invisible and heavenly world, to these? Are they dead,—taken in early ripeness to the gods,—as ancient wisdom foretold their fate? Or did the high idea die out of them, and leave their unperfumed body as its tomb and tablet, announcing to all that the celestial inhabitant, who once gave them beauty,

had departed? Will it be better with the new generation? We
easily predict a fair future to each new candidate who enters the lists, but we are frivolous and volatile, and by low
aims and ill example do what we can to defeat this hope.
Then these youths bring us a rough but effectual aid. By
their unconcealed dissatisfaction, they expose our poverty,
and the insignificance of man to man. A man is a poor lim-
itary benefactor. He ought to be a shower of benefits—a
great influence, which should never let his brother go, but
should refresh old merits continually with new ones; so that,
though absent, he should never be out of my mind, his
name never far from my lips; but if the earth should open
at my side, or my last hour were come, his name should be
the prayer I should utter to the Universe. But in our experience, man is cheap, and friendship wants its deep sense.
We affect to dwell with our friends in their absence, but we
do not; when deed, word, or letter comes not, they let us
go. These exacting children advertise us of our wants. There
is no compliment, no smooth speech with them; they pay
you only this one compliment, of insatiable expectation;
they aspire, they severely exact, and if they only stand fast
in this watch-tower, and persist in demanding unto the end,
and without end, then are they terrible friends, whereof
poet and priest cannot choose but stand in awe; and what
if they eat clouds, and drink wind, they have not been without service to the race of man.

With this passion for what is great and extraordinary, it
cannot be wondered at, that they are repelled by vulgarity
and frivolity in people. They say to themselves, It is better
to be alone than in bad company. And it is really a wish to
be met,—the wish to find society for their hope and reli-

gion,—which prompts them to shun what is called society. They feel that they are never so fit for friendship, as when they have quitted mankind, and taken themselves to friend. A picture, a book, a favorite spot in the hills or the woods, which they can people with the fair and worthy creation of the fancy, can give them often forms so vivid, that these for the time shall seem real, and society the illusion.

But their solitary and fastidious manners not only withdraw them from the conversation, but from the labors of the world; they are not good citizens, not good members of society; unwillingly they bear their part of the public and private burdens; they do not willingly share in the public charities, in the public religious rites, in the enterprises of education, of missions foreign or domestic, in the abolition of the slave-trade, or in the temperance society. They do not even like to vote. The philanthropists inquire whether Transcendentalism does not mean sloth: they had as lief hear that their friend is dead, as that he is a Transcendentalist; for then is he paralyzed, and can never do anything for humanity. What right, cries the good world, has the man of genius to retreat from work, and indulge himself? The popular literary creed seems to be, "I am a sublime genius; I ought not therefore to labor." But genius is the power to labor better and more availably. Deserve thy genius: exalt it. The good, the illuminated, sit apart from the rest, censuring their dulness and vices, as if they thought that, by sitting very grand in their chairs, the very brokers, attorneys, and congressmen would see the error of their ways, and flock to them. But the good and wise must learn to act, and carry salvation to the combatants and demagogues in the dusty arena below.

On the part of these children, it is replied, that life and their faculty seem to them gifts too rich to be squandered on such trifles as you propose to them. What you call your fundamental institutions, your great and holy causes, seem to them great abuses, and, when nearly seen, paltry matters. Each "Cause," as it is called,—say Abolition, Temperance, say Calvinism, or Unitarianism,—becomes speedily a little shop, where the article, let it have been at first never so subtle and ethereal, is now made up into portable and convenient cakes, and retailed in small quantities to suit purchasers. You make very free use of these words "great" and "holy," but few things appear to them such. Few persons have any magnificence of nature to inspire enthusiasm, and the philanthropies and charities have a certain air of quackery. As to the general course of living, and the daily employments of men, they cannot see much virtue in these, since they are parts of this vicious circle; and, as no great ends are answered by the men, there is nothing noble in the arts by which they are maintained. Nay, they have made the experiment, and found that, from the liberal professions to the coarsest manual labor, and from the courtesies of the academy and the college to the conventions of the cotillon-room and the morning call, there is a spirit of cowardly compromise and seeming, which intimates a frightful skepticism, a life without love, and an activity without an aim.

Unless the action is necessary, unless it is adequate, I do not wish to perform it. I do not wish to do one thing but once. I do not love routine. Once possessed of the principle, it is equally easy to make four or forty thousand applications of it. A great man will be content to have indicated in any the slightest manner his perception of the reigning

Idea of his time, and will leave to those who like it the multiplication of examples. When he has hit the white, the rest may shatter the target. Every thing admonishes us how needlessly long life is. Every moment of a hero so raises and cheers us, that a twelve-month is an age. All that the brave Xanthus brings home from his wars, is the recollection that, at the storming of Samos, "in the heat of the battle, Pericles smiled on me, and passed on to another detachment." It is the quality of the moment, not the number of days, of events, or of actors, that imports.

New, we confess, and by no means happy, is our condition: if you want the aid of our labor, we ourselves stand in greater want of the labor. We are miserable with inaction. We perish of rest and rust: but we do not like your work.

"Then," says the world, "show me your own."

"We have none."

"What will you do, then?" cries the world.

"We will wait."

"How long?"

"Until the Universe rises up and calls us to work."

"But whilst you wait, you grow old and useless."

"Be it so: I can sit in a corner and *perish,* (as you call it,) but I will not move until I have the highest command. If no call should come for years, for centuries, then I know that the want of the Universe is the attestation of faith by my abstinence. Your virtuous projects, so called, do not cheer me. I know that which shall come will cheer me. If I cannot work, at least I need not lie. All that is clearly due to-day is not to lie. In other places, other men have encountered sharp trials, and have behaved themselves well. The martyrs were sawn asunder, or hung alive on meat-hooks. Cannot we screw our courage to patience and truth, and without complaint, or even with good-humor, await our turn of action in the Infinite Counsels?"

But, to come a little closer to the secret of these persons, we must say, that to them it seems a very easy matter to answer the objections of the man of the world, but not so easy to dispose of the doubts and objections that occur to themselves. They are exercised in their own spirit with queries, which acquaint them with all adversity, and with the trials of the bravest heroes. When I asked them concerning their private experience, they answered somewhat in this wise: It is not to be denied that there must be some wide difference between my faith and other faith; and mine is a certain brief experience, which surprised me in the highway or in the market, in some place, at some time,—whether in the body or out of the body, God knoweth,—and made me aware that I had played the fool with fools all this time, but that law existed for me and for all; that to me belonged trust, a child's trust and obedience, and the worship of ideas, and I should never be fool more. Well, in the space of an hour, probably, I was let down from this height; I was at my old tricks, the selfish member of a selfish society. My life is superficial, takes no root in the deep world; I ask, When shall I die, and be relieved of the responsibility of seeing an Universe which I do not use? I wish to exchange this flash-of-lightning faith for continuous daylight, this fever-glow for a benign climate.

These two states of thought diverge every moment, and stand in wild contrast. To him who looks at his life from these moments of illumination, it will seem that he skulks and plays a mean, shiftless, and subaltern part in the world.

That is to be done which he has not skill to do, or to be said which others can say better, and he lies by, or occupies his hands with some plaything, until his hour comes again. Much of our reading, much of our labor, seems mere waiting: it was not that we were born for. Any other could do it as well, or better. So little skill enters into these works, so little do they mix with the divine life, that it really signifies little what we do, whether we turn a grindstone, or ride, or run, or make fortunes, or govern the state. The worst feature of this double consciousness is, that the two lives, of the understanding and of the soul, which we lead, really show very little relation to each other, never meet and measure each other: one prevails now, all buzz and din; and the other prevails then, all infinitude and paradise; and, with the progress of life, the two discover no greater disposition to reconcile themselves. Yet, what is my faith? What am I? What but a thought of serenity and independence, an abode in the deep blue sky? Presently the clouds shut down again; yet we retain the belief that this petty web we weave will at last be overshot and reticulated with veins of the blue, and that the moments will characterize the days. Patience, then, is for us, is it not? Patience, and still patience. When we pass, as presently we shall, into some new infinitude, out of this Iceland of negations, it will please us to reflect that, though we had few virtues or consolations, we bore with our indigence, nor once strove to repair it with hypocrisy or false heat of any kind.

But this class are not sufficiently characterized, if we omit to add that they are lovers and worshippers of Beauty. In the eternal trinity of Truth, Goodness, and Beauty, each in its perfection including the three, they prefer to make

Beauty the sign and head. Something of the same taste is observable in all the moral movements of the time, in the religious and benevolent enterprises. They have a liberal, even an aesthetic spirit. A reference to Beauty in action sounds, to be sure, a little hollow and ridiculous in the ears of the old church. In politics, it has often sufficed, when they treated of justice, if they kept the bounds of selfish calculation. If they granted restitution, it was prudence which granted it. But the justice which is now claimed for the black, and the pauper, and the drunkard is for Beauty,—is for a necessity to the soul of the agent, not of the beneficiary. I say, this is the tendency, not yet the realization. Our virtue totters and trips, does not yet walk firmly. Its representatives are austere; they preach and denounce; their rectitude is not yet a grace. They are still liable to that slight taint of burlesque which, in our strange world, attaches to the zealot. A saint should be as dear as the apple of the eye. Yet we are tempted to smile, and we flee from the working to the speculative reformer, to escape that same slight ridicule. Alas for these days of derision and criticism! We call the Beautiful the highest, because it appears to us the golden mean, escaping the dowdiness of the good, and the heartlessness of the true.—They are lovers of nature also, and find an indemnity in the inviolable order of the world for the violated order and grace of man.

There is, no doubt, a great deal of well-founded objection to be spoken or felt against the sayings and doings of this class, some of whose traits we have selected; no doubt, they will lay themselves open to criticism and to lampoons, and as ridiculous stories will be to be told of them as of any. There will be cant and pretension; there will be subtilty and moonshine. These persons are of unequal strength, and do not all prosper. They complain that everything around them must be denied; and if feeble, it takes all their strength to deny, before they can begin to lead their own life. Grave seniors insist on their respect to this institution, and that usage; to an obsolete history; to some vocation, or college, or etiquette, or beneficiary, or charity, or morning or evening call, which they resist, as what does not concern them. But it costs such sleepless nights, alienations and misgivings,— they have so many moods about it;—these old guardians never change *their* minds; they have but one mood on the subject, namely, that Antony is very perverse,—that it is quite as much as Antony can do, to assert his rights, abstain from what he thinks foolish, and keep his temper. He cannot help the reaction of this injustice in his own mind. He is braced-up and stilted; all freedom and flowing genius, all sallies of wit and frolic nature are quite out of the question; it is well if he can keep from lying, injustice, and suicide. This is no time for gaiety and grace. His strength and spirits are wasted in rejection. But the strong spirits overpower those around them without effort. Their thought and emotion comes in like a flood, quite withdraws them from all notice of these carping critics; they surrender themselves with glad heart to the heavenly guide, and only by implication reject the clamorous nonsense of the hour. Grave seniors talk to the deaf,—church and old book mumble and ritualize to an unheeding, preoccupied and advancing mind, and thus they by happiness of greater momentum lose no time, but take the right road at first.

But all these of whom I speak are not proficients; they are novices; they only show the road in which man should travel, when the soul has greater health and prowess. Yet let them feel the dignity of their charge, and deserve a larger power. Their heart is the ark in which the fire is concealed, which shall burn in a broader and universal flame. Let them obey the Genius then most when his impulse is wildest; then most when he seems to lead to uninhabitable desarts of thought and life; for the path which the hero travels alone is the highway of health and benefit to mankind. What is the privilege and nobility of our nature, but its persistency, through its power to attach itself to what is permanent?

Society also has its duties in reference to this class, and must behold them with what charity it can. Possibly some benefit may yet accrue from them to the state. In our Mechanics' Fair, there must be not only bridges, ploughs, carpenters' planes, and baking troughs, but also some few finer instruments,—raingauges, thermometers, and tele-scopes; and in society, besides farmers, sailors, and weavers, there must be a few persons of purer fire kept specially as gauges and meters of character; persons of a fine, detecting instinct, who betray the smallest accumulations of wit and feeling in the bystander. Perhaps too there might be room for the exciters and monitors; collectors of the heavenly spark with power to convey the electricity to others. Or, as the storm-tossed vessel at sea speaks the frigate or "line packet" to learn its longitude, so it may not be without its advantage that we should now and then encounter rare and gifted men, to compare the points of our spiritual compass, and verify our bearings from superior chronometers.

Amidst the downward tendency and proneness of things, when every voice is raised for a new road or another statute, or a subscription of stock, for an improvement in dress, or in dentistry, for a new house or a larger business, for a political party, or the division of an estate,—will you not tolerate one or two solitary voices in the land, speaking for thoughts and principles not marketable or perishable? Soon these improvements and mechanical inventions will be superseded; these modes of living lost out of memory; these cities rotted, ruined by war, by new inventions, by new seats of trade, or the geologic changes:—all gone, like the shells which sprinkle the seabeach with a white colony to-day, forever renewed to be forever destroyed. But the thoughts which these few hermits strove to proclaim by silence, as well as by speech, not only by what they did, but by what they forbore to do, shall abide in beauty and strength, to reorganize themselves in nature, to invest themselves anew in other, perhaps higher endowed and happier mixed clay than ours, in fuller union with the surrounding system.

CIRCLES

Nature centres into balls,
And her proud ephemerals,
Fast to surface and outside,
Scan the profile of the sphere;
Knew they what that signified,
A new genesis were here.

The eye is the first circle; the horizon which it forms is the second; and throughout nature this primary figure is repeated without end. It is the highest emblem in the cipher of the world. St. Augustine described the nature of God as a circle whose centre was everywhere, and its circumference nowhere. We are all our lifetime reading the copious sense of this first of forms. One moral we have already deduced, in considering the circular or compensatory character of every human action. Another analogy we shall now trace; that every action admits of being outdone. Our life is an apprenticeship to the truth, that around every circle another can be drawn; that there is no end in nature, but every end is a beginning; that there is always another dawn risen on mid-noon, and under every deep a lower deep opens.

This fact, as far as it symbolizes the moral fact of the Unattainable, the flying Perfect, around which the hands of man can never meet, at once the inspirer and the condemner of every success, may conveniently serve us to connect many illustrations of human power in every department.

There are no fixtures in nature. The universe is fluid and volatile. Permanence is but a word of degrees. Our globe seen by God is a transparent law, not a mass of facts. The law dissolves the fact and holds it fluid. Our culture is the predominance of an idea which draws after it this train of cities and institutions. Let us rise into another idea: they will disappear. The Greek sculpture is all melted away, as if it had been statues of ice; here and there a solitary figure or fragment remaining, as we see flecks and scraps of snow left in cold dells and mountain clefts, in June and July. For the genius that created it creates now somewhat else. The Greek letters last a little longer, but are already passing under the same sentence, and tumbling into the inevitable pit which the creation of new thought opens for all that is old. The new continents are built out of the ruins of an old planet; the new races fed out of the decomposition of the foregoing. New arts destroy the old. See the investment of capital in aqueducts made useless by hydraulics; fortifications, by gunpowder; roads and canals, by railways; sails, by steam; steam by electricity.

You admire this tower of granite, weathering the hurts of so many ages. Yet a little waving hand built this huge wall, and that which builds is better than that which is built. The hand that built can topple it down much faster. Better than the hand, and nimbler, was the invisible thought which wrought through it; and thus ever, behind the coarse effect, is a fine cause, which, being narrowly seen, is itself the effect of a finer cause. Every thing looks permanent until its secret is known. A rich estate appears to women a firm and lasting fact; to a merchant, one easily created out of any materials, and easily lost. An orchard, good tillage, good grounds, seem a fixture, like a gold mine, or a river, to a citizen; but to a large farmer, not much more fixed than the state of the crop. Nature looks provokingly stable and secular, but it has a cause like all the rest; and when once I comprehend that, will these fields stretch so immovably wide, these leaves hang so individually considerable? Permanence is a word of degrees. Every thing is medial. Moons are no more bounds to spiritual power than bat-balls.

The key to every man is his thought. Sturdy and defying though he look, he has a helm which he obeys, which is the idea after which all his facts are classified. He can only be reformed by showing him a new idea which commands his own. The life of man is a self-evolving circle, which, from a ring imperceptibly small, rushes on all sides outwards to new and larger circles, and that without end. The extent to which this generation of circles, wheel without wheel, will go, depends on the force or truth of the individual soul. For it is the inert effort of each thought, having formed itself into a circular wave of circumstance,—as, for instance, an empire, rules of an art, a local usage, a religious rite,—to heap itself on that ridge, and to solidify and hem in the life. But if the soul is quick and strong, it bursts over that boundary on all sides, and expands another orbit on the great deep, which also runs up into a high wave, with attempt again to stop and to bind. But the heart refuses to be imprisoned; in its first and narrowest pulses, it already tends outward with a vast force, and to immense and innumerable expansions.

Every ultimate fact is only the first of a new series. Every general law only a particular fact of some more general law presently to disclose itself. There is no outside, no inclosing wall, no circumference to us. The man finishes his story,—how good! how final! how it puts a new face on all things! He fills the sky. Lo! on the other side rises also a man, and draws a circle around the circle we had just pronounced the outline of the sphere. Then already is our first speaker not man, but only a first speaker. His only redress is forthwith to draw a circle outside of his antagonist. And so men do by themselves. The result of to-day, which haunts the mind and cannot be escaped, will presently be abridged into a word, and the principle that seemed to explain nature will itself be included as one example of a bolder generalization. In the thought of to-morrow there is a power to upheave all thy creed, all the creeds, all the literatures, of the nations, and marshal thee to a heaven which no epic dream has yet depicted. Every man is not so much a workman in the world, as he is a suggestion of that he should be. Men walk as prophecies of the next age.

Step by step we scale this mysterious ladder: the steps are actions; the new prospect is power. Every several result is threatened and judged by that which follows. Every one seems to be contradicted by the new; it is only limited by the new. The new statement is always hated by the old, and, to those dwelling in the old, comes like an abyss of skepticism. But the eye soon gets wonted to it, for the eye and it are effects of one cause; then its innocency and benefit appear, and presently, all its energy spent, it pales and dwindles before the revelation of the new hour.

Fear not the new generalization. Does the fact look crass and material, threatening to degrade thy theory of spirit? Resist it not; it goes to refine and raise thy theory of matter just as much.

There are no fixtures to men, if we appeal to consciousness. Every man supposes himself not to be fully understood; and if there is any truth in him, if he rests at last on the divine soul, I see not how it can be otherwise. The last chamber, the last closet, he must feel, was never opened; there is always a residuum unknown, unanalyzable. That is, every man believes that he has a greater possibility.

Our moods do not believe in each other. To-day I am full of thoughts, and can write what I please. I see no reason why I should not have the same thought, the same power of expression, to-morrow. What I write, whilst I write it, seems the most natural thing in the world; but yesterday I saw a dreary vacuity in this direction in which now I see so much; and a month hence, I doubt not, I shall wonder who he was that wrote so many continuous pages. Alas for this infirm faith, this will not strenuous, this vast ebb of a vast flow! I am God in nature; I am a weed by the wall.

The continual effort to raise himself above himself, to work a pitch above his last height, betrays itself in a man's relations. We thirst for approbation, yet cannot forgive the approver. The sweet of nature is love; yet, if I have a friend, I am tormented by my imperfections. The love of me accuses the other party. If he were high enough to slight me, then could I love him, and rise by my affection to new heights. A man's growth is seen in the successive choirs of his friends. For every friend whom he loses for truth, he gains a better. I thought, as I walked in the woods and mused on my friends, why should I play with them this game of idolatry? I know and see too well, when not voluntarily blind, the speedy limits of persons called high and worthy. Rich, noble, and great they are by the liberality of our speech, but truth is sad. O blessed Spirit, whom I forsake for these, they are not thou! Every personal consideration that we allow costs us heavenly state. We sell the thrones of angels for a short and turbulent pleasure.

How often must we learn this lesson? Men cease to interest us when we find their limitations. The only sin is limitation. As soon as you once come up with a man's limitations, it is all over with him. Has he talents? has he enterprise? has he knowledge? it boots not. Infinitely alluring and attractive was he to you yesterday, a great hope, a sea to swim in; now, you have found his shores, found it a pond, and you care not if you never see it again.

Each new step we take in thought reconciles twenty seemingly discordant facts, as expressions of one law.

Aristotle and Plato are reckoned the respective heads of two schools. A wise man will see that Aristotle Platonizes. By going one step farther back in thought, discordant opinions are reconciled, by being seen to be two extremes of one principle, and we can never go so far back as to preclude a still higher vision.

Beware when the great God lets loose a thinker on this planet. Then all things are at risk. It is as when a conflagration has broken out in a great city, and no man knows what is safe, or where it will end. There is not a piece of science, but its flank may be turned to-morrow; there is not any literary reputation, not the so-called eternal names of fame, that may not be revised and condemned. The very hopes of man, the thoughts of his heart, the religion of nations, the manners and morals of mankind, are all at the mercy of a new generalization. Generalization is always a new influx of the divinity into the mind. Hence the thrill that attends it.

Valor consists in the power of self-recovery, so that a man cannot have his flank turned, cannot be out-generalled, but put him where you will, he stands. This can only be by his preferring truth to his past apprehension of truth; and his alert acceptance of it, from whatever quarter; the intrepid conviction that his laws, his relations to society, his Christianity, his world, may at any time be superseded and decease.

There are degrees in idealism. We learn first to play with it academically, as the magnet was once a toy. Then we see in the heyday of youth and poetry that it may be true, that it is true in gleams and fragments. Then, its countenance waxes stern and grand, and we see that it must be true. It now shows itself ethical and practical. We learn that God IS that he is in me; and that all things are shadows of him. The idealism of Berkeley is only a crude statement of the idealism of Jesus, and that again is a crude statement of the fact, that all nature is the rapid efflux of goodness executing and organizing itself. Much more obviously is history and the state of the world at any one time directly dependent on the intellectual classification then existing in the minds of men. The things which are dear to men at this hour are so on account of the ideas which have emerged on their mental horizon, and which cause the present order of things as a tree bears its apples. A new degree of culture would instantly revolutionize the entire system of human pursuits.

Conversation is a game of circles. In conversation we pluck up the *termini* which bound the common of silence on every side. The parties are not to be judged by the spirit they partake and even express under this Pentecost. To-morrow they will have receded from this high-water mark. To-morrow you shall find them stooping under the old pack-saddles. Yet let us enjoy the cloven flame whilst it glows on our walls. When each new speaker strikes a new light, emancipates us from the oppression of the last speaker, to oppress us with the greatness and exclusiveness of his own thought, then yields us to another redeemer, we seem to recover our rights, to become men. O, what truths profound and executable only in ages and orbs are supposed in the announcement of every truth! In common hours, society sits cold and statuesque. We all stand waiting, empty,—knowing, possibly, that we can be full, surrounded by mighty symbols which are not symbols to us, but prose and trivial toys. Then cometh the god, and converts the statues into fiery men, and by a flash of his eye burns up the veil which shrouded all things, and the meaning of the very furniture, of cup and saucer, of chair and clock and tester, is manifest. The facts which loomed so large in the fogs of yesterday,—property, climate, breeding, personal beauty, and the like, have strangely changed their proportions.

All that we reckoned settled shakes and rattles; and literatures, cities, climates, religions, leave their foundations, and dance before our eyes. And yet here again see the swift circumspection! Good as is discourse, silence is better, and shames it. The length of the discourse indicates the distance of thought betwixt the speaker and the hearer. If they were at a perfect understanding in any part, no words would be necessary thereon. If at one in all parts, no words would be suffered.

Literature is a point outside of our hodiernal circle, through which a new one may be described. The use of literature is to afford us a platform whence we may command a view of our present life, a purchase by which we may move it. We fill ourselves with ancient learning, install ourselves the best we can in Greek, in Punic, in Roman houses, only that we may wiselier see French, English, and American houses and modes of living. In like manner, we see literature best from the midst of wild nature, or from the din of affairs, or from a high religion. The field cannot be well seen from within the field. The astronomer must have his diameter of the earth's orbit as a base to find the parallax of any star.

Therefore we value the poet. All the argument and all the wisdom is not in the encyclopaedia, or the treatise on metaphysics, or the Body of Divinity, but in the sonnet or the play. In my daily work I incline to repeat my old steps, and do not believe in remedial force, in the power of change and reform. But some Petrarch or Ariosto, filled with the new wine of his imagination, writes me an ode or a brisk romance, full of daring thought and action. He smites and arouses me with his shrill tones, breaks up my whole chain of habits, and I open my eye on my own possibilities. He claps wings to the sides of all the solid old lumber of the world, and I am capable once more of choosing a straight path in theory and practice.

We have the same need to command a view of the religion of the world. We can never see Christianity from the catechism:—from the pastures, from a boat in the pond, from amidst the songs of wood-birds, we possibly may. Cleansed by the elemental light and wind, steeped in the sea of beautiful forms which the field offers us, we may chance to cast a right glance back upon biography. Christianity is rightly dear to the best of mankind; yet was there never a young philosopher whose breeding had fallen into the Christian church, by whom that brave text of Paul's was not specially prized:—"Then shall also the Son be subject unto Him who put all things under him, that God may be all in all." Let the claims and virtues of persons be never so great and welcome, the instinct of man presses eagerly onward to the impersonal and illimitable, and gladly arms itself against the dogmatism of bigots with this generous word out of the book itself.

The natural world may be conceived of as a system of concentric circles, and we now and then detect in nature slight dislocations, which apprize us that this surface on which we now stand is not fixed, but sliding. These manifold tenacious qualities, this chemistry and vegetation, these metals and animals, which seem to stand there for their own sake, are means and methods only,—are words of God, and as fugitive as other words. Has the naturalist or chemist learned his craft, who has explored the gravity of atoms and the elective affinities, who has not yet discerned the deeper law whereof this is only a partial or approximate statement, namely, that like draws to like; and that the goods which belong to you gravitate to you, and need not be pursued with pains and cost? Yet is that statement approximate also, and not final. Omnipresence is a higher fact. Not through subtle, subterranean channels need friend and fact be drawn to their counterpart, but, rightly considered, these things proceed from the eternal generation of the soul. Cause and effect are two sides of one fact.

The same law of eternal procession ranges all that we call the virtues, and extinguishes each in the light of a better. The great man will not be prudent in the popular sense; all his prudence will be so much deduction from his grandeur. But it behooves each to see, when he sacrifices prudence, to what god he devotes it; if to ease and pleasure, he had better be prudent still; if to a great trust, he can well spare his mule and panniers who has a winged chariot instead. Geoffrey draws on his boots to go through the woods, that his feet may be safer from the bite of snakes; Aaron never thinks of such a peril. In many years neither is harmed by such an accident. Yet it seems to me, that, with every precaution you take against such an evil, you put yourself into the power of the evil. I suppose that the highest prudence is the lowest prudence. Is this too sudden a rushing from the centre to the verge of our orbit? Think how many times we shall fall back into pitiful calculations before we take up our rest in the great sentiment, or make the verge of to-day the new centre. Besides, your bravest sentiment is familiar to the humblest men. The poor and the low have their way of expressing the last facts of philosophy as well as you. "Blessed be nothing," and "the worse things are, the better they are," are proverbs which express the transcendentalism of common life.

One man's justice is another's injustice; one man's beauty, another's ugliness; one man's wisdom, another's folly; as one beholds the same objects from a higher point. One man thinks justice consists in paying debts, and has no measure in his abhorrence of another who is very remiss in this duty, and makes the creditor wait tediously. But that second man has his own way of looking at things; asks himself which debt must I pay first, the debt to the rich, or the debt to the poor? the debt of money, or the debt of thought to mankind, of genius to nature? For you, O broker! there is no other principle but arithmetic. For me, commerce is of trivial import; love, faith, truth of character, the aspiration of man, these are sacred; nor can I detach one duty, like you, from all other duties, and concentrate my forces mechanically on the payment of moneys. Let me live onward; you shall find that, though slower, the progress of my character will liquidate all these debts without injustice to higher claims. If a man should dedicate himself to the payment of notes, would not this be injustice? Does he owe no debt but money? And are all claims on him to be postponed to a landlord's or a banker's?

There is no virtue which is final; all are initial. The virtues of society are vices of the saint. The terror of reform is the discovery that we must cast away our virtues, or what we have always esteemed such, into the same pit that has consumed our grosser vices.

"Forgive his crimes, forgive his virtues too, Those smaller faults, half converts to the right."

It is the highest power of divine moments that they abolish our contritions also. I accuse myself of sloth and unprofitableness day by day; but when these waves of God flow into me, I no longer reckon lost time. I no longer poorly compute my possible achievement by what remains to me of the month or the year; for these moments confer a sort of omnipresence and omnipotence which asks nothing of duration, but sees that the energy of the mind is commensurate with the work to be done, without time.

And thus, O circular philosopher, I hear some reader exclaim, you have arrived at a fine Pyrrhonism, at an equivalence and indifferency of all actions, and would fain teach us that, *if we are true,* forsooth, our crimes may be lively stones out of which we shall construct the temple of the true God!

I am not careful to justify myself. I own I am gladdened by seeing the predominance of the saccharine principle throughout vegetable nature, and not less by beholding in morals that unrestrained inundation of the principle of good into every chink and hole that selfishness has left open, yea, into selfishness and sin itself; so that no evil is pure, nor hell itself without its extreme satisfactions. But lest I should mislead any when I have my own head and obey my whims, let me remind the reader that I am only an experimenter. Do not set the least value on what I do, or the least discredit on what I do not, as if I pretended to settle any thing as true or false. I unsettle all things. No facts are to me sacred; none are profane; I simply experiment, an endless seeker, with no Past at my back.

Yet this incessant movement and progression which all things partake could never become sensible to us but by contrast to some principle of fixture or stability in the soul. Whilst the eternal generation of circles proceeds, the eternal generator abides. That central life is somewhat superior to creation, superior to knowledge and thought, and contains all its circles. For ever it labors to create a life and thought as large and excellent as itself; but in vain; for that which is made instructs how to make a better.

Thus there is no sleep, no pause, no preservation, but all things renew, germinate, and spring. Why should we import rags and relics into the new hour? Nature abhors the old, and old age seems the only disease; all others run into this one. We call it by many names,—fever, intemperance, insanity, stupidity, and crime; they are all forms of old age; they are rest, conservatism, appropriation, inertia, not newness, not the way onward. We grizzle every day. I see no need of it. Whilst we converse with what is above us, we do not grow old, but grow young. Infancy, youth, receptive, aspiring, with religious eye looking upward, counts itself nothing, and abandons itself to the instruction flowing from all sides. But the man and woman of seventy assume to know all, they have outlived their hope, they renounce aspiration, accept the actual for the necessary, and talk down to the young. Let them, then, become organs of the Holy Ghost; let them be lovers; let them behold truth; and their eyes are uplifted, their wrinkles smoothed, they are perfumed again with hope and power. This old age ought not to creep on a human mind. In nature every moment is new; the past is always swallowed and forgotten; the coming only is sacred. Nothing is secure but life, transition, the energizing spirit. No love can be bound by oath or covenant to secure it against a higher love. No truth so sublime but it may be trivial to-morrow in the light of new thoughts. People wish to be settled; only as far as they are unsettled is there any hope for them.

Life is a series of surprises. We do not guess to-day the mood, the pleasure, the power of to-morrow, when we are building up our being. Of lower states,—of acts of routine and sense,—we can tell somewhat; but the masterpieces of God, the total growths and universal movements of the soul, he hideth; they are incalculable. I can know that truth is divine and helpful; but how it shall help me I can have no guess, for *so to be* is the sole inlet of *so to know.* The new position of the advancing man has all the powers of the old, yet has them all new. It carries in its bosom all the energies of the past, yet is itself an exhalation of the morning. I cast away in this new moment all my once hoarded knowledge, as vacant and vain. Now, for the first time, seem I to know any thing rightly. The simplest words,—we do not know what they mean, except when we love and aspire.

The difference between talents and character is adroitness to keep the old and trodden round, and power and courage to make a new road to new and better goals. Character makes an overpowering present; a cheerful, determined hour, which fortifies all the company, by making them see that much is possible and excellent that was not thought of. Character dulls the impression of particular events. When we see the conqueror, we do not think much of any one battle or success. We see that we had exaggerated the difficulty. It was easy to him. The great man is not convulsible or tormentable; events pass over him without much impression. People say sometimes, "See what I have overcome; see how cheerful I am; see how completely I have triumphed over these black events." Not if they still remind me of the black event. True conquest is the causing the calamity to fade and disappear, as an early cloud of insignificant result in a history so large and advancing.

The one thing which we seek with insatiable desire is to forget ourselves, to be surprised out of our propriety, to lose our sempiternal memory, and to do something without knowing how or why; in short, to draw a new circle. Nothing great was ever achieved without enthusiasm. The way of life is wonderful: it is by abandonment. The great moments of history are the facilities of performance through the strength of ideas, as the works of genius and religion. "A man," said Oliver Cromwell, "never rises so high as when he knows not whither he is going." Dreams and drunkenness, the use of opium and alcohol are the semblance and counterfeit of this oracular genius, and hence their dangerous attraction for men. For the like reason, they ask the aid of wild passions, as in gaming and war, to ape in some manner these flames and generosities of the heart.

FREDERIC HENRY HEDGE

In "Questionings," Hedge entertains the notions of the world as "mind," with a nod to the implications of such a view. Is the world an illusion? Is the moon there in reality if I am not look-

ing at it? The last stanza resolves the conundrum while it retains
the mystery.

QUESTIONINGS

Hath this world, without me wrought,
Other substance than my thought?
Lives it by my sense alone,
Or by essence of its own?
Will its life, with mine begun,
Cease to be when that is done,
Or another consciousness
With the self-same forms impress?

Doth yon fireball, poised in air,
Hang by my permission there?
Are the clouds that wander by,
But the offspring of mine eye,
Born with every glance I cast,
Perishing when that is past?
And those thousand, thousand eyes,
Scattered through the twinkling skies,
Do they draw their life from mine,
Or, of their own beauty shine?

Now I close my eyes, my ears,
And creation disappears,
Yet if I but speak the word,
All creation is restored.

Or—more wonderful – within,
New creations do begin;
Hues more bright and forms more rare,
Than reality doth wear,
Flash across my inward sense,
Born of the mind's omnipotence.

Soul! that all informest, say!
Shall these glories pass away?
Will those planets cease to blaze,
When these eyes no longer gaze?
And the life of things be o'er,
When these pulses beat no more?

Thought! that in me works and lives,—
Life to all things living gives,—
Art thy not thyself, perchance,
But the universe in trance?
A reflection inly flung
By that world thou fanciedst sprung
From myself;—thyself a dream;—
Of the world's thinking thou the theme.

Be it thus, or be thy birth
From a source above the earth.
Be thou matter, be thou mind,
In thee alone myself I find,
And through thee alone, for me,
Hath this world reality.
Therefore, in thee will I live,
To thee all myself will give,

Losing still, that I may find,
This bounded self in boundless mind.

AMOS BRONSON ALCOTT

Aside from his "Orphic Sayings" and the transcribed *Conversations with Children,* the best writing from Alcott's own hand comes from his extensive journals. His writing here is more direct, less ornate and thus more revealing. In particular, the journal for 1837 gives an account of that challenging year, as he sought to hold on to his school, to publish his work, and to establish firm relations with the other Transcendentalists, particularly Emerson.

JOURNAL ENTRIES, 1837

The lecture of Mr. Emerson on Thursday evening of this week was on Religion. . . . The speaker always kindles a sublime sentiment when, in those deep and oracular undertones which he knows when and how to use, he speaks of the divine entities of all being. A solemn and supernatural awe creeps over one as the serene pathos of his manner and the unaffected earnestness of his bearing come upon the senses. Here, I think, lies Emerson's power. At long intervals of remark bordering almost on coarseness—now the tones that he weaves into his diction and the pictures of vulgar life that he draws with a Shakespearean boldness of delineation depicting farmers, tradesmen, beasts, vermin, the rabid mob, the courtesan, the under as well as the upper vulgar, and now sliding into all that is beautiful, refined, elegant, both in thought, speech, action, and vocation—he bursts upon the hearers in strains of thought and charm and diction that affect the soul by their bewildering loftiness and grandeur. The burlesque is, in a twinkling, transformed into the serious. The bold and sketchy outline becomes a deep and sublime idea. This is the poet's, not the logician's, power.

His ideas are clothed in bold, sharp, natural images. He states, pictures, sketches, but does not reason. His appeal is through the imagination and the senses to the mind. He leaves things in the place in which Nature put them, never deranging that order for a special logical analysis. All his ideas come orbed and winged. Footed and creeping things stand in contrast to give them effect; nor do slime and puddles become insignificant or unworthy in his creation. They occupy their place, as in great nature, serving as types and contrasts to the clean and solid ground of ideas. Nature shines serenely through the calm depths of his soul, and leaves upon its unruffled surface the images of all her works. . . .

The day shall come when this man's genius shall shine beyond the circle of his own city and nation. He shall flash across the wide water and receive the homage of other peoples. Emerson is destined to be the high literary name of this age. Other men we have who chaffer in the nooks and corners of this wide sea, and whose wares are peddled in this place and that; but this man's genius is cosmopolitan, and shall be in demand wherever man has risen above the mere mechanics and utilities of life. A race of more worthy artists shall take the place of our present vulgar artisans, and clean and tasteful products shall spring from their labours. Our hawkers of letters and writers by brain-force shall yield to regal and honorable booksellers, and these shall be served by artists who know the spirit that is given them, and will not trade it in the market or profane it by vulgar toil.

And much do we need this purification of the temple of literature. Emerson's whip of small cords—delicate and subtle of speech, eloquent with truth—shall do somewhat to drive the buyers and sellers of slang and profanity from the sacred place, and the nation reap fruits of his honorable daring in a regenerate and tasteful literature, free from sordid interests, sectarian cant, and the shallowness of a godless philosophy. Honorable-notion and sham-image killer is he! Up-turner of all time-worn and vulgar associations thickly strewn over the soil of our land, now all exposed to the light of day by his shining and driving share. Drive on thy team, young and hopeful artist, till not ever a stone or sod shall not have been presented in a new aspect and new relation to the radiant orb of day! Break up the old and effete ground, and sow lavishly the seeds of new and refreshing nature, that thus, in due time, a rich spiritual harvest may be gathered and garnered!'

January, Week IV
He that seeks not to affix things external to the soul, to subordinate the shows of nature to the Ideas of the Spirit, doeth nought. His life is a waste. "He liveth in a vain show and disquieteth himself in vain." To the soul are space and time given not as adding aught to its indwelling treasures, for it is richer and fuller than these phenomena, but to serve and honor it. Space is the soul's workshop, and Time is its work-

day while incarnate and plying organic instruments. The soul humbles itself, takes upon itself the frail and finite flesh with all its infirmities; it descendeth from its high throne to lift matter into the light of its presence. . . .

Man is God conditioned, God subdivided from himself in order to look backward upon himself. He that doth not believe himself a God hath lost all sense, all remembrance of his Father. He is an outcast from the paternal mansion, an orphan and forlorn. He is not, as was the tender and loving Jesus, identified with the Father, and hath no consciousness of his immortal relation. He dieth, in his thought, when his body deserts him. He maketh the body, indeed, himself. He liveth in matter. He is matter, for the idea of the Spirit hath quite died out of him—and when that which his mind knoweth vanisheth, what has he to hold his nature?

February, Week VIII

A great good is always done to a man when he shall be led to distrust the truth of the opinions and the fitness of the age in which he lives. Men should fight against their own age, inasmuch as the work which they have to do is always in it, and whatever honorable name they shall obtain, of lasting good which they shall effect for their race, is to be achieved by overcoming the evils of their time. A man's work is always in the present, and whether he shall live thereafter and become a part of all time ends on the fact of his knowing his age and marrying all is best and worthy in it with all other time—and this his lot to serve by reforming the evils peculiar to it, and thus, revealing the eternal truths and principles which these overlie obscure.

February, Week IX

Dr. Channing's efforts have been put forth to good purpose on many occasions—always, however, by way of quieting and allaying. He never makes an Idea; but, after these have begun to work and have put the public mind into action, then does he give his assent to them—usually, however, with so much compromise and timid modification, lest he should stir up the fears and passions of conservatives, that much of their good effect is lost. Dr. Channing always has the last word to say, never the first. Hence he gets the credit of wisdom which belongs of right to those who have set this wisdom afloat in a community, and opened the eyes of men.

April, Week XV

It is much to have the vision of the seeing eye. Did most men possess this, the useful hand would be empowered with new dexterity also. Emerson sees me, knows me, and, more than all others, helps me—not by noisy praise, not by vain appeals to interest and passion, but by turning the eyes of others to my stand in reason and things.

This has been a week of few incidents, but of sober reflection. An unusual degree of excitement has pervaded this metropolis regarding my book. I have been severely censured. I have come by friends to my enterprise who respect my character for the publication of this work. At one time the excitement threatened a mob. The plan was to make the assault at one of my Friday evening Conversations. But no such outrage was attempted, and the minds of the disaffected are now settling into quietude.

Such a state of feeling calls for serious reflection. I have, of course, been much exercised in this way. What my future movements shall be, time must decide. At present, I see not my way. The only course which, as a man of honor and dignity, I can pursue is to preserve unbroken silence on this subject, inasmuch as I have committed no offence nor stepped from the line of my duty.

April, Week XVI

Though my mind has been deeply and earnestly intent on the aspects of the time during this week, I have committed but few thoughts or accounts of circumstances to this paper. This is not the hour to record the permanent and real, while the sense looks forth on little save the apparent and tangible. Forms are now, instead of substance. Things overlie and shut out ideas. The popular soul is an idolater. I would not prostrate myself in this worship of the outward, but retire reverently within, and commune in quietude and silence with the divine forces of the common Being whereof all men are emanations.

April, Week XVII

Doth a man desire to be alone in this wide domain of the terrestrial? Doth he wish to shut himself from the approaches of his kind, and bear a solitary nature on the earth? Then shall he do this on one condition: let him reflect! Let him commune with his own Soul! So shall he outstrip and outlive the race of his contemporaries, and find companionship with the great and wise of bygone centuries as the reward of his toil. Thought severs a man from his age. It beggars him of sympathy, to enrich him with the friendship of all prior intellects. It unfits him for falling in with the notions of his time. It lifts him from the dust and smoke of the present action and interests into the clear and untroubled vision of the future.

May, Week XVIII

I took a short walk with Mr. Ripley during this week. I am pleased to find him so cordial. He seems to enter the movements of the time with not a little of interest and intelligence. Of the ministers of this city he is, perhaps, the most in favor of fair and free discussion. He tells me that his brethren have been considering the subject of freedom of discussion at their weekly meetings during their last two sittings, and that they have been led to it by the manner in which my book has been spoken of, and my enterprise, in the public prints. From him I learn that these gentlemen, with a few exceptions, regard me as an interloper into the theological field, and deem this a fit occasion to make their sentiments known. They do not countenance my speculations, nor look with friendly eyes on my enterprise. Besides this, the teachers of public schools in this city, owing to the freedom of remarks in which I indulge or to the present state of education among us, owe me no good will, and here a favorable moment has come for a movement against me. There is already a strong sentiment unfriendly to me and my purpose. But amidst this are most worthy and wise advocates of my principles and course. Neither the ministers nor the teachers, with their allies, can, I fancy, defeat my plans.

May, Week XIX

Among other things, in his letter of this week Emerson has the following: In the few moments' broken conversation I had with *you* a fortnight ago, it seems to me *you* did not acquiesce at all in what is always my golden view for *you,* as for all men to whom God has given the "vision and faculty divine"; namely, that one day *you* would leave the impracticable world to wag on its own way, and sit apart and write your oracles for its behoof. Write! Let them hear or let them forbear; the written word abides, until *slowly* and unexpectedly and in widely sundered places it has created its own church. And my love and confidence in that silent Muse is such that, in circumstances in which I can easily conceive myself placed, I should prefer some manual or quite mechanical labour as a means of living that should leave me a few sacred hours in the twenty-four, to any attempts *to* realize my idea in any existing forms called intellectual or spiritual, where, by defying every settled usage of society, I should be sure *to sour* my *own* temper.

My friend sympathizes more intensely in my speculative than in my practical genius. I would fain give my powers fit exercise in each of these modes of action. I would realize and embody my idea as fully as my time shall suffer. Still it may be that the speculative more than the practical element preponderates in me, and that it were wiser to obey my friend. Time shall decide for me.

May, Week XX

I spent a few days with Mr. Emerson at his own house in Concord. . . . Little difference of opinion seemed to exist between us. The means and method of communication with the age were the chief points of difference. Emerson, true to his genius, favors written works. He holds men and things at a distance, pleases himself with using them for his own benefit and as means of gathering materials for his works. He does not believe in the actual. His sympathies are all intellectual. He persuades me to leave the actual, devote myself to the speculative, and embody my thoughts in written works. . . .

Emerson idealizes all things. This idealized picture is the true and real one to him. All else is nought. Even persons are thus idealized, and his interest in them and their influence over him exists no longer than this conformity appears in his imagination. Beauty, beauty—this it is that charms him. But beauty has pure and delicate tastes, and hence all that mars or displeases this sense, with however much of truth or of interest it may be associated, is of no interest to his mind. Emerson seeks the beauty of truth: it is not so much a quest of truth in itself as the beauty thereof; not so much the desire of being holy and true as of setting forth in fit and graceful terms the beauty of truth and holiness. With him, all men and things have a beauty; but this is the result of his point of vision, and often falls wide of the actual truth. To give pleasure more than to impart truth is his mission. What is beautiful in man, nature, or art—this he apprehends, and with the poet's power sets forth.

His genius is high and commanding. He will do honour to his age. As a man, however, this visit has somewhat modified my former notions of him. He seems not to be fully in earnest. He writes and speaks for effect. Fame stands before him as a dazzling award, and he holds himself somewhat too proudly, nor seeks the humble and sincere regard of his race. His life has been one of opportunity, and he has sought to realize in it more of the accomplished scholar than the perfect man.—A great intellect, refined by elegant study, rather than a divine life radiant with the beauty of truth and holiness. He is an eye more than a heart, an intellect more than a soul.

May, Week XXI

I wrote a letter to Emerson, apprising him of the proposed meeting of like minds on Monday next, at Rev. Mr. Ripley's. These meetings, given to conversation on topics of high moment, were deemed quite profitable as well as interesting when last held, during the summer and autumn of 1836. We purpose to renew them. The following gentlemen are expected to attend:

These gentlemen are all intent on advancing the honor and interests of humanity. They comprise the few among us that take higher and diviner views of the soul than men have been wont to take in past times. They incline to the spiritual doctrines, each taking his own view of subjects. We propose to meet and disclose to each other our views and purposes—to receive and impart light, if light we have among us to confer. I value this opportunity as one of benefit to myself. It puts me in possession of the current genius of the time, acquaints me with its cherished purposes and means of action, and thus brings my own mind in communion with its co-mates.

November, Week XLIV

I call that man no wise Christian who belies the divinity of his nature by denying the identity of his soul with God. I deem his creed false to the spirit of his master's teachings. He ever declared the union of his own soul with God, and, as constantly, denied all superiority of nature above others. I pronounce the man that sees not this intimate and divine union yet destitute of the spirit of his master, and a vilifier of his holy religion. For this debases the eternity of the soul and the dignity of man's nature. I say that the Christian world is anti-Christ.

November, Week XLV

Thus, day by day, amidst this hour of small profit in the actual, do I live. Circumstances, age, do not favor such work as I have to do. Only, or chiefly, do I live in Idea. I order my life before mine own eyes and those of my household, but the age will not employ me. I am an Idea without hands. I find no body for my thought amidst the materials of this age. It denies me timber. What shall I do but content myself with my lot, and await in patience the hour when the age shall give work for my faculties and honor my art, supplying materials therefore—when souls shall be proffered instead of bodies, and I shall practice my art on these, moulding them into figures of beauty by wise discipline?

Complain not then, my genius. Thou shalt know thyself in fit time, and do thy deed before the ages. Ply well thy faculties. Thou mayest fit thyself by wise self-insight, by study of the time, for future toil when the age shall have reason to see thy purpose. This shall one day approach thee, now at a distance. Wait thou, and watch its tardy steps. Study its signs. Question it. Chide it.

November, Week XLV

Let a thorough scholar—a man whose nature has not been stolen away by precedent of books, but who sees man ever above and of more value than the speech he employs—let such a man leave the conventional city, wherein nature, having profaned herself, is ashamed to acknowledge her misdeeds but sinks these out of hearing in speech, and visit a rural retreat of simple people. Let him mark their speech, observe their manners. Shall he not find himself again in the presence of his proper nature, of which the city had well-nigh bereft him?

These people put themselves into their speech. They do not hide their souls. Words are things with them. Their souls slide over their tongues. They are not hutched within and hidden from sight. And in this simple, free state of being their language is more true to nature. They speak it in greater purity than the artificial citizen or closeted bookworm. It is nearer to the soul, and the vocabulary of speech is wider at the same time that it is more faithful to the soul. I never hear a countryman speak without being reminded of the dignity of our common nature and the richness of our common tongue. He reminds me of Shakespeare. He has retained his epithets. Language appears in its simpler, worthier forms. He deals with its staples. Its great words slip from his tongue. The needs of the soul shine in his speech. His vocabulary is not shorn of woods, winds, waters, sky, toil, humanity. It hath a soul in it. Its images are of God's shaping. It deals in the product of nature, and shames art—save when she, like him, is faithful to the uses and ends of nature. I would rather study simple countryman amidst the scenes of nature, as dictionary of my native tongue, than commune with citizen amidst his conventions, or read with professor in college or hall, the tomes of a library. There is life and meaning in it. It is devoid of pretense. It is mother tongue.

Now I am visibly idle. My hand is without service. The age hath no work for me. I stand with folded arms, desirous of doing some service for soul; but the age hath nothing of that sort on hand. . . . Unheeded, I gaze on labourers around me. All hands, how busy! What noise of instruments! What roar of elements!

"Fool!" saith all the age, "didst thou think the soul, of which thou talkest and for which wouldst fain labour even unto death, hath aught like this? Thou speakest, mystically, of instincts, faculties, whose needs these arts shall never supply. Behold, all Nature labours and lends her stores to supply all needs."

November, Week XLVII (on his birthday)
This year has been one of trial. It has been rich in discipline, and has done me good. I have been thrown upon my own resources, and have found these. My faculties have been sharpened for work. I have had much of self-insight, have learned the dignity of standing alone before my age. Experience thus precious I have cause to regard with thankfulness. Doubtless the year upon which I now enter shall be equally rich in means of self-discipline, and my faculties strengthened by the events through which it shall conduct me.

Save me, O ye destinies, from idleness, from tame and servile engagements, from compliance with the vulgar aims and pursuits of my age! Lift me above its low maxims, and

make me a light shining amidst darkness! So shall my year
be one of blessing and reward.

MARGARET FULLER

The poem entitled "Flaxman" is a tribute to John Flaxman
(1755–1826), well-known British sculptor, friend of William
Blake, and supporter of the Platonist Thomas Taylor, whose translations were influential in Transcendental circles. The poem illustrates the power of art to differentiate the several faculties of
perception within the human instrument, symbolized in the poem
by the "daily self" and the "truest self."

FLAXMAN

We deemed the secret lost, the spirit gone,
Which spake in Greek simplicity of thought,
And in the forms of gods and heroes wrought
Eternal beauty from the sculptured stone
A higher charm than modern culture won,
With all the wealth of metaphysic lore,
Gifted to analyze, dissect, explore.
A many-colored light flows from our sun;
Art, 'neath its beams, a motley thread has spun;
The prison modifies the perfect day;
But thou hast known such mediums to shun,
And cast once more on life a pure white ray.
Absorbed in the creations of thy mind,
Forgetting daily self, my truest self I find.

For Fuller, the theme of marriage symbolized both the role of women in society and the various stages in spiritual progress. The poem "The Sacred Marriage" develops the theme of opening doors to higher knowledge through the gate of a shared life. Her advice: hide nothing and work together toward a greater unity. The following prose passage, excerpted from "The Great Lawsuit," illustrates again, through marriage, the various stages of enlightenment in a life lived consciously.

THE SACRED MARRIAGE

And has another's life as large a scope?
It may give due fulfilment to thy hope,
And every portal to the unknown may ope.

If, near this other life, thy inmost feeling
Trembles with fateful prescience of revealing
The future Deity, time is still concealing.

If thou feel thy whole force drawn more and more
To launch that other bark on seas without a shore;
And no still secret must be kept in store;

If meannesses that dim each temporal deed,
The dull decay that mars the fleshly weed,
And flower of love that seems to fall and leave no seed

Hide never the full presence from thy sight
Of mutual aims and tasks, ideals bright,
Which feed their roots to-day on all this seeming blight.

Twin stars that mutual circle in the heaven,
Two parts for spiritual concord given,
Twin Sabbaths that inlock the Sacred Seven;

Still looking to the centre for the cause,
Mutual light giving to draw out the powers,
And learning all the other groups by cognizance of one
   another's laws:

The parent love the wedded love includes,
The one permits the two their mutual moods,
The two each other know mid myriad multitudes;

With child-like intellect discerning love,
And mutual action energizing love,
In myriad forms affiliating love.

A world whose seasons bloom from pole to pole,
A force which knows both starting-point and goal,
A home in heaven,—the Union in the soul.

EXCERPT FROM "THE GREAT LAWSUIT: MAN VERSUS MEN. WOMAN VERSUS WOMEN." (*THE DIAL*, 1843)

Centuries have passed since, but civilized Europe is still in a transition state about marriage, not only in practice, but in thought. A great majority of societies and individuals are still doubtful whether earthly marriage is to be a union of souls, or merely a contract of convenience and utility. Were woman established in the rights of an immortal being, this could not be. She would not in some countries be given away by her father, with scarcely more respect for her own feelings than is shown by the Indian chief, who sells his daughter for a horse, and beats her if she runs away from her new home. Nor, in societies where her choice is left free, would she be perverted, by the current of opinion that seizes her, into the belief that she must marry, if it be only to find a protector, and a home of her own.

Neither would man, if he thought that the connection was of permanent importance, enter upon it so lightly. He would not deem it a trifle, that he was to enter into the closest relations with another soul, which, if not eternal in themselves, must eternally affect his growth.

Neither, did he believe woman capable of friendship, would he, by rash haste, lose the chance of finding a friend in the person who might, probably, live half a century by his side. Did love to his mind partake of infinity, he would not miss his chance of its revelations, that he might the sooner rest from his weariness by a bright fireside, and have a sweet and graceful attendant, "devoted to him alone." Were he a step higher, he would not carelessly enter into a relation, where he might not be able to do the duty of a friend, as well as a protector from external ill, to the other party, and have a being in his power pining for sympathy, intelligence, and aid, that he could not give.

Where the thought of equality has become pervasive, it shows itself in four kinds.

The household partnership. In our country the woman looks for a "smart but kind" husband, the man for a "capable, sweet-tempered" wife.

The man furnishes the house, the woman regulates it.

Their relation is one of mutual esteem, mutual dependence. Their talk is of business, their affection shows itself by practical kindness. They know that life goes more smoothly and cheerfully to each for the other's aid; they are grateful and content. The wife praises her husband as a "good provider," the husband in return compliments her as a "capital housekeeper." This relation is good as far as it goes.

Next comes a closer tie which takes the two forms, either of intellectual companionship, or mutual idolatry. The last, we suppose, is to no one a pleasing subject of contemplation. The parties weaken and narrow one another; they lock the gate against all the glories of the universe that they may live in a cell together. To themselves they seem the only wise, to all others steeped in infatuation, the gods smile as they look forward to the crisis of cure, to men the woman seems an unlovely syren, to women the man an effeminate boy.

The other form, of intellectual companionship, has become more and more frequent. Men engaged in public life, literary men, and artists have often found in their wives companions and confidants in thought no less than in feeling. And, as in the course of things the intellectual development of woman has spread wider and risen higher, they have, not unfrequently, shared the same employment. As in the case of Roland and his wife, who were friends in the household and the nation's councils, read together, regulated home affairs, or prepared public documents together indifferently.

It is very pleasant, in letters begun by Roland and finished by his wife, to see the harmony of mind and the difference of nature, one thought, but various ways of treating it. This is one of the best instances of a marriage of friendship. It was only friendship, whose basis was esteem; probably neither party knew love, except by name. Roland was a good man, worthy to esteem and be esteemed, his wife as deserving of admiration as able to do without it. Madame Roland is the fairest specimen we have yet of her class, as clear to discern her aim, as valiant to pursue it, as Spenser's Britomart, austerely set apart from all that did not belong to her, whether as woman or as mind. She is an antetype of a class to which the coming time will afford a field, the Spartan matron, brought by the culture of a book-furnishing age to intellectual consciousness and expansion.

Self-sufficing strength and clear-sightedness were in her combined with a power of deep and calm affection. The page of her life is one of unsullied dignity.

Her appeal to posterity is one against the injustice of those who committed such crimes in the name of liberty. She makes it in behalf of herself and her husband. I would put beside it on the shelf a little volume, containing a similar appeal from the verdict of contemporaries to that of mankind, that of Godwin in behalf of his wife, the celebrated, the by most men detested Mary Wollstonecraft. In his view it was an appeal from the injustice of those who did such wrong in the name of virtue.

Were this little book interesting for no other cause, it would be so for the generous affection evinced under the peculiar circumstances. This man had courage to love and honor this woman in the face of the world's verdict, and of all that was repulsive in her own past history. He believed he saw of what soul she was, and that the thoughts she had struggled to act out were noble. He loved her and he defended her for the meaning and intensity of her inner life. It was a good fact.

Mary Wollstonecraft, like Lucie Dudevant (commonly known as George Sand) in our day, was a woman whose existence better proved the need of some new interpretation of woman's rights, than anything she wrote. Such women as these, rich in genius, of most tender sympathies, and capable of high virtue and a chastened harmony, ought not to find themselves by birth in a place so narrow, that in breaking bonds they become outlaws. Were there as much room in the world for such, as in Spenser's poem for Britomart, they would not run their heads so wildly against its laws. They find their way at last to purer air, but the world will not take off the brand it has set upon them. The champion of the rights of woman found in Godwin, one who pleads her own cause like a brother. George Sand smokes, wears male attire, wishes to be addressed as Mon frere; perhaps, if she found those who were as brothers indeed, she would not care whether she were brother or sister.

We rejoice to see that she, who expresses such a painful contempt for men in most of her works, as shows she must have known great wrong from them, in La Roche Mauprat depicting one raised, by the workings of love, from the depths of savage sensualism to a moral and intellectual life. It was love for a pure object, for a steadfast woman, one of those who, the Italian said, could make the stair to heaven.

Women like Sand will speak now, and cannot be silenced; their characters and their eloquence alike foretell an era when such as they shall easier learn to lead true lives. But though such forebode, not such shall be the parents of it.

Those who would reform the world must show that they do not speak in the heat of wild impulse; their lives must be unstained by passionate error; they must be severe lawgivers to themselves. As to their transgressions and opinions, it may be observed, that the resolve of Eloisa to be only the mistress of Abelard, was that of one who saw the contract of marriage a seal of degradation. Wherever abuses of this sort are seen, the timid will suffer, the bold protest. But society is in the right to outlaw them till she has revised her law, and she must be taught to do so, by one who speaks with authority, not in anger and haste.

If Godwin's choice of the calumniated authoress of the "Rights of Woman," for his honorod wife, be a sign of a new era, no less so is an article of great learning and eloquence, published several years since in an English review, where the writer, in doing full justice to Eloisa, shows his bitter regret that she lives not now to love him, who might have known better how to prize her love than did the egotistical Abelard.

These marriages, these characters, with all their imperfections, express an onward tendency. They speak of aspiration of soul, of energy of mind, seeking clearness and freedom. Of a like promise are the tracts now publishing by Goodwyn Barmby (the European Pariah as he calls himself) and his wife Catharine. Whatever we may think of their measures, we see them in wedlock, the two minds are wed by the only contract that can permanently avail, of a common faith, and a common purpose.

We might mention instances, nearer home, of minds, partners in work and in life, sharing together, on equal terms, public and private interests, and which have not on any side that aspect of offence which characterizes the attitude of the last named; persons who steer straight onward, and in our freer life have not been obliged to run their heads against any wall. But the principles which guide them might, under petrified or oppressive institutions, have made them warlike, paradoxical, or, in some sense, Pariahs. The phenomenon is different, the law the same, in all these cases. Men and women have been obliged to build their house from the very foundation. If they found stone ready in the quarry, they took it peaceably, otherwise they alarmed the country by pulling down old towers to get materials.

These are all instances of marriage as intellectual companionship. The parties meet mind to mind, and a mutual trust is excited which can buckler them against a million. They work together for a common purpose, and, in all these instances, with the same implement, the pen.

A pleasing expression in this kind is afforded by the union in the names of the Howitts. William and Mary Howitt we heard named together for years, supposing them to be brother and sister; the equality of labors and reputation, even so, was auspicious, more so, now we find them man and wife. In his late work on Germany, Howitt mentions his wife with pride, as one among the constellation of distinguished English women, and in a graceful, simple manner.

In naming these instances we do not mean to imply that community of employment is an essential to union of this sort, more than to the union of friendship. Harmony exists no less in difference than in likeness, if only the same keynote govern both parts. Woman the poem, man the poet; woman the heart, man the head; such divisions are only important when they are never to be transcended. If nature is never bound down, nor the voice of inspiration stifled, that is enough. We are pleased that women should write and speak, if they feel the need of it, from having something to tell; but silence for a hundred years would be as well, if that silence be from divine command, and not from man's tradition.

HENRY DAVID THOREAU

Walden fuses reflection and observation so smoothly that we are seldom conscious of the mind at work. In the chapters "Where I Lived, and What I Lived For," and "Conclusion," however, Thoreau is more explicit about his sojourn at the pond, speaking directly to the reader. They contain some of the more oft-quoted passages in the book. The last section, "Conclusion," perhaps sermonizes to excess, but serves in its way to look back at the experience from the distance of Thoreau's return to "civilization." By the time he wrote this, the cabin had been sold and removed from the site.

WHERE I LIVED, AND WHAT I LIVED FOR

At a certain season of our life we are accustomed to consider every spot as the possible site of a house. I have thus surveyed the country on every side within a dozen miles of where I live. In imagination I have bought all the farms in succession, for all were to be bought, and I knew their price. I walked over each farmer's premises, tasted his wild apples, discoursed on husbandry with him, took his farm at his price, at any price, mortgaging it to him in my mind; even put a higher price on it—took everything but a deed of it—took his word for his deed, for I dearly love to talk—cultivated it, and him too to some extent, I trust, and withdrew when I had enjoyed it long enough, leaving him to carry it on. This experience entitled me to be regarded as a sort of real-estate broker by my friends. Wherever I sat, there I might live, and the landscape radiated from me accordingly. What is a house but a sedes, a seat?—better if a country seat. I discovered many a site for a house not likely to be soon improved, which some might have thought too far from the village, but to my eyes the village was too far from it. Well, there I might live, I said; and there I did live, for an hour, a summer and a winter life; saw how I could let the years run off, buffet the winter through, and see the spring come in. The future inhabitants of this region, wherever they may place their houses, may be sure that they have been anticipated. An afternoon sufficed to lay out the land into orchard, wood-lot, and pasture, and to decide what fine oaks or pines should be left to stand before the door, and whence each blasted tree could be seen to the best advantage; and then I let it lie, fallow, perchance, for a man is rich in proportion to the number of things which he can afford to let alone.

My imagination carried me so far that I even had the refusal of several farms—the refusal was all I wanted—but I never got my fingers burned by actual possession. The nearest that I came to actual possession was when I bought the Hollowell place, and had begun to sort my seeds, and collected materials with which to make a wheelbarrow to carry it on or off with; but before the owner gave me a deed of it, his wife—every man has such a wife—changed her mind and wished to keep it, and he offered me ten dollars to release him. Now, to speak the truth, I had but ten cents in the world, and it surpassed my arithmetic to tell, if I was that man who had ten cents, or who had a farm, or ten dollars, or all together. However, I let him keep the ten dollars and the farm too, for I had carried it far enough; or rather, to be generous, I sold him the farm for just what I gave for it, and, as he was not a rich man, made him a present of ten dollars, and still had my ten cents, and seeds, and materials for a wheelbarrow left. I found thus that I had been a rich man without any damage to my poverty. But I retained the landscape, and I have since annually carried off what it yielded without a wheelbarrow. With respect to landscapes,

> *"I am monarch of all I survey,*
> *My right there is none to dispute."*

I have frequently seen a poet withdraw, having enjoyed the most valuable part of a farm, while the crusty farmer supposed that he had got a few wild apples only. Why, the owner does not know it for many years when a poet has put his farm in rhyme, the most admirable kind of invisible fence, has fairly impounded it, milked it, skimmed it, and got all the cream, and left the farmer only the skimmed milk.

The real attractions of the Hollowell farm, to me, were: its complete retirement, being, about two miles from the village, half a mile from the nearest neighbor, and separated from the highway by a broad field; its bounding on the river, which the owner said protected it by its fogs from frosts in the spring, though that was nothing to me; the gray color and ruinous state of the house and barn, and the dilapidated fences, which put such an interval between me and the last occupant; the hollow and lichen-covered apple trees, gnawed by rabbits, showing what kind of neighbors I should have; but above all, the recollection I had of it from my earliest voyages up the river, when the house was concealed behind a dense grove of red maples, through which I heard the house-dog bark. I was in haste to buy it, before the proprietor finished getting out some rocks, cutting down the hollow apple trees, and grubbing up some young birches which had sprung up in the pasture, or, in short, had made any more of his improvements. To enjoy these advantages I was ready to carry it on; like Atlas, to take the world on my shoulders—I never heard what compensation he received for that—and do all those things which had no other motive or excuse but that I might pay for it and be unmolested in my possession of it; for I knew all the while that it would yield the most abundant crop of the kind I wanted, if I could only afford to let it alone. But it turned out as I have said.

All that I could say, then, with respect to farming on a large scale—I have always cultivated a garden—was, that I had had my seeds ready. Many think that seeds improve with age. I have no doubt that time discriminates between the good and the bad; and when at last I shall plant, I shall be less likely to be disappointed. But I would say to my fellows, once for all, As long as possible live free and uncommitted. It makes but little difference whether you are committed to a farm or the county jail.

Old Cato, whose "De Re Rustica" is my "Cultivator," says—and the only translation I have seen makes sheer nonsense of the passage—"When you think of getting a farm turn it thus in your mind, not to buy greedily; nor spare your pains to look at it, and do not think it enough to go round it once. The oftener you go there the more it will please you, if it is good." I think I shall not buy greedily, but go round and round it as long as I live, and be buried in it first, that it may please me the more at last.

The present was my next experiment of this kind, which I purpose to describe more at length, for convenience putting the experience of two years into one. As I have said, I do not propose to write an ode to dejection, but to brag as lustily as chanticleer in the morning, standing on his roost, if only to wake my neighbors up.

When first I took up my abode in the woods, that is, began to spend my nights as well as days there, which, by accident, was on Independence Day, or the Fourth of July, 1845, my house was not finished for winter, but was merely a defence against the rain, without plastering or chimney, the walls being of rough, weather-stained boards, with wide chinks, which made it cool at night. The upright white hewn studs and freshly planed door and window casings gave it a clean and airy look, especially in the morning, when its timbers were saturated with dew, so that I fancied that by noon some sweet gum would exude from them. To my imagination it retained throughout the day more or less of this auroral character, reminding me of a certain house on a mountain which I had visited a year before. This was an airy and unplastered cabin, fit to entertain a travelling god, and where a goddess might trail her garments. The winds which passed over my dwelling were such as sweep over the ridges of mountains, bearing the broken strains, or celestial parts only, of terrestrial music. The morning wind forever blows, the poem of creation is uninterrupted; but few are the ears that hear it. Olympus is but the outside of the earth every where.

The only house I had been the owner of before, if I except a boat, was a tent, which I used occasionally when making excursions in the summer, and this is still rolled up in my garret; but the boat, after passing from hand to hand, has gone down the stream of time. With this more substantial shelter about me, I had made some progress toward settling in the world. This frame, so slightly clad, was a sort of crystallization around me, and reacted on the builder. It was suggestive somewhat as a picture in outlines. I did not need to go outdoors to take the air, for the atmosphere within had lost none of its freshness. It was not so much within doors as behind a door where I sat, even in the rainiest weather. The *Harivansa* says, "An abode without birds is like a meat without seasoning." Such was not my abode, for I found myself suddenly neighbor to the birds; not by having imprisoned one, but having caged myself near them. I was not only nearer to some of those which commonly frequent the garden and the orchard, but to those smaller and more thrilling songsters of the forest which never, or rarely, serenade a villager—the wood thrush, the veery, the scarlet tanager, the field sparrow, the whippoorwill, and many others.

I was seated by the shore of a small pond, about a mile and a half south of the village of Concord and somewhat higher than it, in the midst of an extensive wood between that town and Lincoln, and about two miles south of that our only field known to fame, Concord Battle Ground; but I was so low in the woods that the opposite shore, half a mile off, like the rest, covered with wood, was my most distant horizon. For the first week, whenever I looked out on the pond it impressed me like a tarn high up on the side of a mountain, its bottom far above the surface of other lakes, and, as the sun arose, I saw it throwing off its nightly clothing of mist, and here and there, by degrees, its soft ripples or its smooth reflecting surface was revealed, while the mists, like ghosts, were stealthily withdrawing in every direction into the woods, as at the breaking up of some nocturnal conventicle. The very dew seemed to hang upon the trees later into the day than usual, as on the sides of mountains.

This small lake was of most value as a neighbor in the intervals of a gentle rain-storm in August, when, both air and water being perfectly still, but the sky overcast, mid-afternoon had all the serenity of evening, and the wood thrush sang around, and was heard from shore to shore. A lake like this is never smoother than at such a time; and the clear portion of the air above it being, shallow and darkened by clouds, the water, full of light and reflections, becomes a lower heaven itself so much the more important. From a hill-top near by, where the wood had been recently cut off, there was a pleasing vista southward across the pond, through a wide indentation in the hills which form the shore there, where their opposite sides sloping toward each other suggested a stream flowing out in that direction through a wooded valley, but stream there was none. That way I looked between and over the near green hills to some distant and higher ones in the horizon, tinged with blue.

Indeed, by standing on tiptoe I could catch a glimpse of some of the peaks of the still bluer and more distant mountain ranges in the northwest, those true-blue coins from heaven's own mint, and also of some portion of the village. But in other directions, even from this point, I could not see over or beyond the woods which surrounded me. It is well to have some water in your neighborhood, to give buoyancy to and float the earth. One value even of the smallest well is, that when you look into it you see that earth is not continent but insular. This is as important as that it keeps butter cool. When I looked across the pond from this peak toward the Sudbury meadows, which in time of flood I distinguished elevated perhaps by a mirage in their seething valley, like a coin in a basin, all the earth beyond the pond appeared like a thin crust insulated and floated even by this small sheet of interverting water, and I was reminded that this on which I dwelt was but dry land.

Though the view from my door was still more contracted, I did not feel crowded or confined in the least. There was pasture enough for my imagination. The low shrub oak plateau to which the opposite shore arose stretched away toward the prairies of the West and the steppes of Tartary, affording ample room for all the roving families of men. "There are none happy in the world but beings who enjoy freely a vast horizon"—said Damodara, when his herds required new and larger pastures.

Both place and time were changed, and I dwelt nearer to those parts of the universe and to those eras in history which had most attracted me. Where I lived was as far off as many a region viewed nightly by astronomers. We are wont to imagine rare and delectable places in some remote and more celestial corner of the system, behind the constellation of Cassiopeia's Chair, far from noise and disturbance. I discovered that my house actually had its site in such a withdrawn, but forever new and unprofaned, part of the universe. If it were worth the while to settle in those parts near to the Pleiades or the Hyades, to Aldebaran or Altair, then I was really there, or at an equal remoteness from the life which I had left behind, dwindled and twinkling with as fine a ray to my nearest neighbor, and to be seen only in moonless nights by him. Such was that part of creation where I had squatted,—

"There was a shepherd that did live,
And held his thoughts as high
As were the mounts whereon his flocks
Did hourly feed him by."

What should we think of the shepherd's life if his flocks always wandered to higher pastures than his thoughts?

Every morning was a cheerful invitation to make my life of equal simplicity, and I may say innocence, with Nature herself. I have been as sincere a worshipper of Aurora as the Greeks. I got up early and bathed in the pond; that was a religious exercise, and one of the best things which I did. They say that characters were engraven on the bathing tub of King Tching Thang to this effect: "Renew thyself completely each day; do it again, and again, and forever again." I can understand that. Morning brings back the heroic ages. I was as much affected by the faint hum of a mosquito making its invisible and unimaginable tour through my apartment at earliest dawn, when I was sitting with door and windows open, as I could be by any trumpet that ever sang of fame. It was Homer's requiem; itself an Iliad and Odyssey in the air, singing its own wrath and wanderings. There was something cosmical about it; a standing advertisement, till forbidden, of the everlasting vigor and fertility of the world. The morning, which is the most memorable season of the day, is the awakening hour. Then there is least somnolence in us; and for an hour, at least, some part of us awakes which slumbers all the rest of the day and night. Little is to be expected of that day, if it can be called a day, to which we are not awakened by our Genius, but by the mechanical nudgings of some servitor, are not awakened by our own newly acquired force and aspirations from within, accompanied by the undulations of celestial music, instead of factory bells, and a fragrance filling the air—to a higher life than we fell asleep from; and thus the darkness bear its fruit, and prove itself to be good, no less than the light. That man who does not believe that each day contains an earlier, more sacred, and auroral hour than he has yet profaned, has despaired of life, and is pursuing a descending and darkening way. After a partial cessation of his sensuous life, the soul of man, or its organs rather, are reinvigorated each day, and his Genius tries again what noble life it can make. All memorable events, I should say, transpire in morning time and in a morning atmosphere. The Vedas say, "All intelligences awake with the morning." Poetry and art, and the fairest and most memorable of the actions of men, date from such an hour. All poets and heroes, like Memnon, are the children of Aurora, and emit their music at sunrise. To him whose elastic and vigorous thought keeps pace with the sun, the day is a perpetual morning. It matters not what the clocks say or the attitudes and labors of men. Morning is when I am awake and there is a dawn in me. Moral reform is the effort to throw off sleep. Why is it that men give so poor an account of their day if they have not been slumbering? They are not such poor calculators. If they had not been overcome with drowsiness, they would have performed something. The millions are awake enough for physical labor; but only one in a million is awake enough for effective intellectual exertion, only one in a hundred millions to a poetic or divine life. To be awake is to be alive. I have never yet met a man who was quite awake. How could I have looked him in the face?

We must learn to reawaken and keep ourselves awake, not by mechanical aids, but by an infinite expectation of the dawn, which does not forsake us in our soundest sleep. I know of no more encouraging fact than the unquestionable ability of man to elevate his life by a conscious endeavor. It is something to be able to paint a particular picture, or to carve a statue, and so to make a few objects beautiful; but it is far more glorious to carve and paint the very atmosphere and medium through which we look, which morally we can do. To affect the quality of the day, that is the highest of arts. Every man is tasked to make his life, even in its details, worthy of the contemplation of his most elevated and critical hour. If we refused, or rather used up, such paltry information as we get, the oracles would distinctly inform us how this might be done.

I went to the woods because I wished to live deliberately, to front only the essential facts of life, and see if I could not learn what it had to teach, and not, when I came to die, discover that I had not lived. I did not wish to live

what was not life, living is so dear; nor did I wish to practise resignation, unless it was quite necessary. I wanted to
live deep and suck out all the marrow of life, to live so stur-
dily and Spartan-like as to put to rout all that was not life,
to cut a broad swath and shave close, to drive life into a corner, and reduce it to its lowest terms, and, if it proved to be
mean, why then to get the whole and genuine meanness of
it, and publish its meanness to the world; or if it were sublime, to know it by experience, and be able to give a true account of it in my next excursion. For most men, it appears
to me, are in a strange uncertainty about it, whether it is of
the devil or of God, and have somewhat hastily concluded
that it is the chief end of man here to "glorify God and
enjoy him forever."

Still we live meanly, like ants; though the fable tells us
that we were long ago changed into men; like pygmies we
fight with cranes; it is error upon error, and clout upon
clout, and our best virtue has for its occasion a superfluous
and evitable wretchedness. Our life is frittered away by detail. An honest man has hardly need to count more than his
ten fingers, or in extreme cases he may add his ten toes, and
lump the rest. Simplicity, simplicity, simplicity! I say, let
your affairs be as two or three, and not a hundred or a thousand; instead of a million count half a dozen, and keep your
accounts on your thumb-nail. In the midst of this chopping
sea of civilized life, such are the clouds and storms and
quicksands and thousand-and-one items to be allowed for,
that a man has to live, if he would not founder and go to
the bottom and not make his port at all, by dead reckon-
ing, and he must be a great calculator indeed who succeeds.
Simplify, simplify. Instead of three meals a day, if it be nec-

essary eat but one; instead of a hundred dishes, five; and reduce other things in proportion. Our life is like a German
Confederacy, made up of petty states, with its boundary
forever fluctuating, so that even a German cannot tell you
how it is bounded at any moment. The nation itself, with
all its so-called internal improvements, which, by the way
are all external and superficial, is just such an unwieldy and
overgrown establishment, cluttered with furniture and
tripped up by its own traps, ruined by luxury and heedless
expense, by want of calculation and a worthy aim, as the
million households in the land; and the only cure for it, as
for them, is in a rigid economy, a stern and more than
Spartan simplicity of life and elevation of purpose. It lives
too fast. Men think that it is essential that the Nation have
commerce, and export ice, and talk through a telegraph,
and ride thirty miles an hour, without a doubt, whether
they do or not; but whether we should live like baboons or
like men, is a little uncertain. If we do not get out sleepers,
and forge rails, and devote days and nights to the work, but
go to tinkering upon our lives to improve them, who will
build railroads? And if railroads are not built, how shall we
get to heaven in season? But if we stay at home and mind
our business, who will want railroads? We do not ride on the
railroad; it rides upon us. Did you ever think what those
sleepers are that underlie the railroad? Each one is a man,
an Irishman, or a Yankee man. The rails are laid on them,
and they are covered with sand, and the cars run smoothly
over them. They are sound sleepers, I assure you. And every
few years a new lot is laid down and run over; so that, if
some have the pleasure of riding on a rail, others have the
misfortune to be ridden upon. And when they run over a

man that is walking in his sleep, a supernumerary sleeper in the wrong position, and wake him up, they suddenly stop the cars, and make a hue and cry about it, as if this were an exception. I am glad to know that it takes a gang of men for every five miles to keep the sleepers down and level in their beds as it is, for this is a sign that they may sometime get up again.

Why should we live with such hurry and waste of life? We are determined to be starved before we are hungry. Men say that a stitch in time saves nine, and so they take a thousand stitches today to save nine tomorrow. As for work, we haven't any of any consequence. We have the Saint Vitus' dance, and cannot possibly keep our heads still. If I should only give a few pulls at the parish bell-rope, as for a fire, that is, without setting the bell, there is hardly a man on his farm in the outskirts of Concord, notwithstanding that press of engagements which was his excuse so many times this morning, nor a boy, nor a woman, I might almost say, but would forsake all and follow that sound, not mainly to save property from the flames, but, if we will confess the truth, much more to see it burn, since burn it must, and we, be it known, did not set it on fire—or to see it put out, and have a hand in it, if that is done as handsomely; yes, even if it were the parish church itself. Hardly a man takes a half-hour's nap after dinner, but when he wakes he holds up his head and asks, "What's the news?" as if the rest of mankind had stood his sentinels. Some give directions to be waked every half-hour, doubtless for no other purpose; and then, to pay for it, they tell what they have dreamed. After a night's sleep the news is as indispensable as the breakfast. "Pray tell me anything new that has happened to a man anywhere on this globe"—and he reads it over his coffee and rolls, that a man has had his eyes gouged out this morning on the Wachito River; never dreaming the while that he lives in the dark unfathomed mammoth cave of this world, and has but the rudiment of an eye himself.

For my part, I could easily do without the post-office. I think that there are very few important communications made through it. To speak critically, I never received more than one or two letters in my life—I wrote this some years ago—that were worth the postage. The penny-post is, commonly, an institution through which you seriously offer a man that penny for his thoughts which is so often safely offered in jest. And I am sure that I never read any memorable news in a newspaper. If we read of one man robbed, or murdered, or killed by accident, or one house burned, or one vessel wrecked, or one steamboat blown up, or one cow run over on the Western Railroad, or one mad dog killed, or one lot of grasshoppers in the winter—we never need read of another. One is enough. If you are acquainted with the principle, what do you care for a myriad instances and applications? To a philosopher all news, as it is called, is gossip, and they who edit and read it are old women over their tea. Yet not a few are greedy after this gossip. There was such a rush, as I hear, the other day at one of the offices to learn the foreign news by the last arrival, that several large squares of plate glass belonging to the establishment were broken by the pressure—news which I seriously think a ready wit might write a twelve-month, or twelve years, beforehand with sufficient accuracy. As for Spain, for instance, if you know how to throw in Don Carlos and the Infanta, and Don Pedro and Seville and Granada, from time to time in the right proportions—they may have changed the names a little since I saw the papers—and serve up a bull-fight when other entertainments fail, it will be true to the letter, and give us as good an idea of the exact state or ruin of things in Spain as the most succinct and lucid reports under this head in the newspapers: and as for England, almost the last significant scrap of news from that quarter was the revolution of 1649; and if you have learned the history of her crops for an average year, you never need attend to that thing again, unless your speculations are of a merely pecuniary character. If one may judge who rarely looks into the newspapers, nothing new does ever happen in foreign parts, a French revolution not excepted.

What news! how much more important to know what that is which was never old! "Kieou-he-yu (great dignitary of the state of Wei) sent a man to Khoung-tseu to know his news. Khoung-tseu caused the messenger to be seated near him, and questioned him in these terms: What is your master doing? The messenger answered with respect: My master desires to diminish the number of his faults, but he cannot accomplish it. The messenger being gone, the philosopher remarked: What a worthy messenger! What a worthy messenger!" The preacher, instead of vexing the ears of drowsy farmers on their day of rest at the end of the week—for Sunday is the fit conclusion of an ill-spent week, and not the fresh and brave beginning of a new one—with this one other draggle-tail of a sermon, should shout with thundering voice, "Pause! Avast! Why so seeming fast, but deadly slow?"

Shams and delusions are esteemed for soundest truths, while reality is fabulous. If men would steadily observe realities only, and not allow themselves to be deluded, life, to compare it with such things as we know, would be like a fairy tale and the Arabian Nights' Entertainments. If we respected only what is inevitable and has a right to be, music and poetry would resound along the streets. When we are unhurried and wise, we perceive that only great and worthy things have any permanent and absolute existence, that petty fears and petty pleasures are but the shadow of the reality. This is always exhilarating and sublime. By closing the eyes and slumbering, and consenting to be deceived by shows, men establish and confirm their daily life of routine and habit everywhere, which still is built on purely illusory foundations. Children, who play life, discern its true law and relations more clearly than men, who fail to live it worthily, but who think that they are wiser by experience, that is, by failure. I have read in a Hindoo book, that "there was a king's son, who, being expelled in infancy from his native city, was brought up by a forester, and, growing up to maturity in that state, imagined himself to belong to the barbarous race with which he lived. One of his father's ministers having discovered him, revealed to him what he was, and the misconception of his character was removed, and he knew himself to be a prince. So soul," continues the Hindoo philosopher, "from the circumstances in which it is placed, mistakes its own character, until the truth is revealed to it by some holy teacher, and then it knows itself to be Brahma." I perceive that we inhabitants of New England live this mean life that we do because our vision does not penetrate the surface of things. We think that that is which appears to be. If a man should walk through this town and see only the reality, where, think you, would the "Mill-dam" go to? If he should give us an account of the realities he beheld there, we should not recognize the place in his description. Look at a meeting-house, or a court-house, or a jail, or a shop, or a dwelling-house, and say what that thing really is before a true gaze, and they would all go to pieces in your account of them. Men esteem truth remote, in the outskirts of the system, behind the farthest star, before Adam and after the last man. In eternity there is indeed something true and sublime. But all these times and places and occasions are now and here. God himself culminates in the present moment, and will never be more divine in the lapse of all the ages. And we are enabled to apprehend at all what is sublime and noble only by the perpetual instilling and drenching of the reality that surrounds us. The universe constantly and obediently answers to our conceptions; whether we travel fast or slow, the track is laid for us. Let us spend our lives in conceiving then. The poet or the artist never yet had so fair and noble a design but some of his posterity at least could accomplish it.

Let us spend one day as deliberately as Nature, and not be thrown off the track by every nutshell and mosquito's wing that falls on the rails. Let us rise early and fast, or break fast, gently and without perturbation; let company come and let company go, let the bells ring and the children cry—determined to make a day of it. Why should we knock under and go with the stream? Let us not be upset and overwhelmed in that terrible rapid and whirlpool called a dinner, situated in the meridian shallows. Weather this danger and you are safe, for the rest of the way is down hill. With unrelaxed nerves, with morning vigor, sail by it, looking another way, tied to the mast like Ulysses. If the engine whistles, let it whistle till it is hoarse for its pains. If the bell rings, why should we run? We will consider what kind of music they are like. Let us settle ourselves, and work and wedge our feet downward through the mud and slush of opinion, and prejudice, and tradition, and delusion, and appearance, that alluvion which covers the globe, through Paris and London, through New York and Boston and Concord, through Church and State, through poetry and philosophy and religion, till we come to a hard bottom and rocks in place, which we can call reality, and say, This is, and no mistake; and then begin, having a point d'appui, below freshet and frost and fire, a place where you might found a wall or a state, or set a lamp-post safely, or perhaps a gauge, not a Nilometer, but a Realometer, that future ages might know how deep a freshet of shams and appearances had gathered from time to time. If you stand right fronting and face to face to a fact, you will see the sun glimmer on both its surfaces, as if it were a cimeter, and feel its sweet edge dividing you through the heart and marrow, and so you will happily conclude your mortal career. Be it life or death, we crave only reality. If we are really dying, let us hear the rattle in our throats and feel cold in the extremities; if we are alive, let us go about our business.

Time is but the stream I go a-fishing in. I drink at it; but while I drink I see the sandy bottom and detect how shallow it is. Its thin current slides away, but eternity remains. I would drink deeper; fish in the sky, whose bottom is pebbly with stars. I cannot count one. I know not the first letter of the alphabet. I have always been regretting that I was not as wise as the day I was born. The intellect is a cleaver; it discerns and rifts its way into the secret of things. I do not wish to be any more busy with my hands than is necessary. My head is hands and feet. I feel all my best faculties concentrated in it. My instinct tells me that my head is an organ for burrowing, as some creatures use their snout and fore paws, and with it I would mine and burrow my way through these hills. I think that the richest vein is somewhere hereabouts; so by the divining-rod and thin rising vapors I judge; and here I will begin to mine.

CONCLUSION

To the sick the doctors wisely recommend change of air and scenery. Thank Heaven, here is not all the world. The buckeye does not grow in New England, and the mockingbird is rarely heard here. The wild goose is more of a cosmopolite than we; he breaks his fast in Canada, takes a luncheon in the Ohio, and plumes himself for the night in a southern bayou. Even the bison, to some extent, keeps pace with the seasons cropping the pastures of the Colorado only till a greener and sweeter grass awaits him by the Yellowstone. Yet we think that if rail fences are pulled down, and stone walls piled up on our farms, bounds are henceforth set to our lives and our fates decided. If you are chosen town clerk, forsooth, you cannot go to Tierra del Fuego this summer: but you may go to the land of infernal fire nevertheless. The universe is wider than our views of it.

Yet we should oftener look over the tafferel of our craft, like curious passengers, and not make the voyage like stupid sailors picking oakum. The other side of the globe is but the home of our correspondent. Our voyaging is only great-circle sailing, and the doctors prescribe for diseases of the skin merely. One hastens to southern Africa to chase the giraffe; but surely that is not the game he would be after. How long, pray, would a man hunt giraffes if he could? Snipes and woodcocks also may afford rare sport; but I trust it would be nobler game to shoot one's self.—

> *"Direct your eye right inward, and you'll find*
> *A thousand regions in your mind*
> *Yet undiscovered. Travel them, and be*
> *Expert in home-cosmography."*

What does Africa—what does the West stand for? Is not our own interior white on the chart? black though it may prove, like the coast, when discovered. Is it the source of the Nile, or the Niger, or the Mississippi, or a Northwest Passage around this continent, that we would find? Are these the problems which most concern mankind? Is Franklin the only man who is lost, that his wife should be so earnest to find him? Does Mr. Grinnell know where he himself is? Be rather the Mungo Park, the Lewis and Clark and Frobisher, of your own streams and oceans; explore your own higher latitudes—with shiploads of preserved meats to support you, if they be necessary; and pile the empty cans sky-high for a sign. Were preserved meats invented to preserve meat merely? Nay, be a Columbus to whole new continents and worlds within you, opening new channels, not of trade, but of thought. Every man is the lord of a realm beside which the earthly empire of the Czar is but a petty state, a hummock left by the ice. Yet some can be patriotic who have no self-respect, and sacrifice the greater to the less. They love the soil which makes their graves, but have no sympathy with the spirit which may still animate their clay. Patriotism is a maggot in their heads. What was the meaning of that South-Sea Exploring Expedition, with all its parade and expense, but an indirect recognition of the fact that there are continents and seas in the moral world to which every man is an isthmus or an inlet, yet unexplored by him, but that it is easier to sail many thousand miles through cold and storm and cannibals, in a government ship, with five hundred men and boys to assist one, than it is to explore the private sea, the Atlantic and Pacific Ocean of one's being alone.

> "Erret, et extremos alter scrutetur Iberos.
> Plus habet hic vitae, plus habet ille viae."

> Let them wander and scrutinize the outlandish Australians.
> I have more of God, they more of the road.

It is not worth the while to go round the world to count the cats in Zanzibar. Yet do this even till you can do better, and you may perhaps find some "Symmes' Hole" by which to get at the inside at last. England and France, Spain and Portugal, Gold Coast and Slave Coast, all front on this private sea; but no bark from them has ventured out of sight of land, though it is without doubt the direct way to India. If you would learn to speak all tongues and conform to the customs of all nations, if you would travel farther than all travellers, be naturalized in all climes, and cause the Sphinx to dash her head against a stone, even obey the precept of the old philosopher, and Explore thyself. Herein are demanded the eye and the nerve. Only the defeated and deserters go to the wars, cowards that run away and enlist. Start now on that farthest western way, which does not pause at the Mississippi or the Pacific, nor conduct toward a wornout China or Japan, but leads on direct, a tangent to this sphere, summer and winter, day and night, sun down, moon down, and at last earth down too.

It is said that Mirabeau took to highway robbery "to ascertain what degree of resolution was necessary in order to place one's self in formal opposition to the most sacred laws of society." He declared that "a soldier who fights in the ranks does not require half so much courage as a footpad"— "that honor and religion have never stood in the way of a well-considered and a firm resolve." This was manly, as the world goes; and yet it was idle, if not desperate. A saner man would have found himself often enough "in formal opposition" to what are deemed "the most sacred laws of society," through obedience to yet more sacred laws, and so have tested his resolution without going out of his way. It is not for a man to put himself in such an attitude to society, but to maintain himself in whatever attitude he find himself through obedience to the laws of his being, which will never be one of opposition to a just government, if he should chance to meet with such.

I left the woods for as good a reason as I went there. Perhaps it seemed to me that I had several more lives to live, and could not spare any more time for that one. It is remarkable how easily and insensibly we fall into a particular route, and make a beaten track for ourselves. I had not lived there a week before my feet wore a path from my door to the pond-side; and though it is five or six years since I trod it, it is still quite distinct. It is true, I fear, that others may have fallen into it, and so helped to keep it open. The surface of the earth is soft and impressible by the feet of men; and so with the paths which the mind travels. How worn and dusty, then, must be the highways of the world, how deep the ruts of tradition and conformity! I did not wish to take a cabin passage, but rather to go before the mast and on the deck of the world, for there I could best see the moonlight amid the mountains. I do not wish to go below now.

I learned this, at least, by my experiment: that if one advances confidently in the direction of his dreams, and endeavors to live the life which he has imagined, he will meet with a success unexpected in common hours. He will put some things behind, will pass an invisible boundary; new, universal, and more liberal laws will begin to establish themselves around and within him; or the old laws be expanded, and interpreted in his favor in a more liberal sense, and he will live with the license of a higher order of beings. In proportion as he simplifies his life, the laws of the universe will appear less complex, and solitude will not be solitude, nor poverty poverty, nor weakness weakness. If you have built castles in the air, your work need not be lost; that is where they should be. Now put the foundations under them.

It is a ridiculous demand which England and America make, that you shall speak so that they can understand you. Neither men nor toadstools grow so. As if that were important, and there were not enough to understand you without them. As if Nature could support but one order of understandings, could not sustain birds as well as quadrupeds, flying as well as creeping things, and hush and whoa, which Bright can understand, were the best English. As if there were safety in stupidity alone. I fear chiefly lest my expression may not be extra-vagant enough, may not wander far enough beyond the narrow limits of my daily experience, so as to be adequate to the truth of which I have been convinced. Extra vagance! it depends on how you are yarded. The migrating buffalo, which seeks new pastures in another latitude, is not extravagant like the cow which kicks over the pail, leaps the cowyard fence, and runs after her calf, in milking time. I desire to speak somewhere without bounds; like a man in a waking moment, to men in their waking moments; for I am convinced that I cannot exaggerate enough even to lay the foundation of a true expression. Who that has heard a strain of music feared then lest he should speak extravagantly any more forever? In view of the future or possible, we should live quite laxly and undefined in front, our outlines dim and misty on that side; as our shadows reveal an insensible perspiration toward the sun. The volatile truth of our words should continually betray the inadequacy of the residual statement. Their truth is instantly translated; its literal monument alone remains. The words which express our faith and piety are not definite; yet they are significant and fragrant like frankincense to superior natures.

Why level downward to our dullest perception always, and praise that as common sense? The commonest sense is the sense of men asleep, which they express by snoring. Sometimes we are inclined to class those who are once-and-a-half-witted with the half-witted, because we appreciate only a third part of their wit. Some would find fault with the morning red, if they ever got up early enough. "They pretend," as I hear, "that the verses of Kabir have four different senses; illusion, spirit, intellect, and the exoteric doctrine of the Vedas"; but in this part of the world it is considered a ground for complaint if a man's writings admit of more than one interpretation. While England endeavors to cure the potato-rot, will not any endeavor to cure the brain-rot, which prevails so much more widely and fatally?

I do not suppose that I have attained to obscurity, but I should be proud if no more fatal fault were found with my pages on this score than was found with the Walden ice. Southern customers objected to its blue color, which is the evidence of its purity, as if it were muddy, and preferred the Cambridge ice, which is white, but tastes of weeds. The purity men love is like the mists which envelop the earth, and not like the azure ether beyond.

Some are dinning in our ears that we Americans, and moderns generally, are intellectual dwarfs compared with the ancients, or even the Elizabethan men. But what is that to the purpose? A living dog is better than a dead lion. Shall a man go and hang himself because he belongs to the race of pygmies, and not be the biggest pygmy that he can? Let every one mind his own business, and endeavor to be what he was made.

Why should we be in such desperate haste to succeed and in such desperate enterprises? If a man does not keep pace with his companions, perhaps it is because he hears a different drummer. Let him step to the music which he hears, however measured or far away. It is not important that he should mature as soon as an apple tree or an oak. Shall he turn his spring into summer? If the condition of things which we were made for is not yet, what were any reality which we can substitute? We will not be shipwrecked on a vain reality. Shall we with pains erect a heaven of blue glass over ourselves, though when it is done we shall be sure to gaze still at the true ethereal heaven far above, as if the former were not?

There was an artist in the city of Kouroo who was disposed to strive after perfection. One day it came into his mind to make a staff. Having considered that in an imperfect work time is an ingredient, but into a perfect work time does not enter, he said to himself, It shall be perfect in all respects, though I should do nothing else in my life. He proceeded instantly to the forest for wood, being resolved that it should not be made of unsuitable material; and as he searched for and rejected stick after stick, his friends gradually deserted him, for they grew old in their works and died, but he grew not older by a moment. His singleness of purpose and resolution, and his elevated piety, endowed him, without his knowledge, with perennial youth. As he made no compromise with Time, Time kept out of his way, and only sighed at a distance because he could not overcome him. Before he had found a stick in all respects suitable the city of Kouroo was a hoary ruin, and he sat on one of its mounds to peel the stick. Before he had given it the proper shape the dynasty of the Candahars was at an end, and with the point of the stick he wrote the name of the last of that race in the sand, and then resumed his work. By the time he had smoothed and polished the staff Kalpa was no longer the pole-star; and ere he had put on the ferule and the head adorned with precious stones, Brahma had awoke and slumbered many times. But why do I stay to mention these things? When the finishing stroke was put to his work, it suddenly expanded before the eyes of the astonished artist into the fairest of all the creations of Brahma. He had made a new system in making a staff, a world with full and fair proportions; in which, though the old cities and dynasties had passed away, fairer and more glorious ones had taken their places. And now he saw by the heap of shavings still fresh at his feet, that, for him and his work, the former lapse of time had been an illusion, and that no more time had elapsed than is required for a single scintillation from the brain of Brahma to fall on and inflame the tinder of a mortal brain. The material was pure, and his art was pure; how could the result be other than wonderful?

No face which we can give to a matter will stead us so well at last as the truth. This alone wears well. For the most part, we are not where we are, but in a false position. Through an infinity of our natures, we suppose a case, and put ourselves into it, and hence are in two cases at the same time, and it is doubly difficult to get out. In sane moments we regard only the facts, the case that is. Say what you have to say, not what you ought. Any truth is better than make-believe. Tom Hyde, the tinker, standing on the gallows, was asked if he had anything to say. "Tell the tailors," said he, "to remember to make a knot in their thread before they take the first stitch." His companion's prayer is forgotten.

However mean your life is, meet it and live it; do not shun it and call it hard names. It is not so bad as you are. It looks poorest when you are richest. The fault-finder will find faults even in paradise. Love your life, poor as it is. You may perhaps have some pleasant, thrilling, glorious hours, even in a poorhouse. The setting sun is reflected from the windows of the almshouse as brightly as from the rich man's abode; the snow melts before its door as early in the spring.

I do not see but a quiet mind may live as contentedly there, and have as cheering thoughts, as in a palace. The town's poor seem to me often to live the most independent lives of any. Maybe they are simply great enough to receive without misgiving. Most think that they are above being supported by the town; but it oftener happens that they are not above supporting themselves by dishonest means, which should be more disreputable. Cultivate poverty like a garden herb, like sage. Do not trouble yourself much to get new things, whether clothes or friends. Turn the old; return to them. Things do not change; we change. Sell your clothes and keep your thoughts. God will see that you do not want society. If I were confined to a corner of a garret all my days, like a spider, the world would be just as large to me while I had my thoughts about me. The philosopher said: "From an army of three divisions one can take away its general, and put it in disorder; from the man the most abject and vulgar one cannot take away his thought." Do not seek so anxiously to be developed, to subject yourself to many influences to be played on; it is all dissipation. Humility like darkness reveals the heavenly lights. The shadows of poverty and meanness gather around us, "and lo! creation widens to our view." We are often reminded that if there were bestowed on us the wealth of Croesus, our aims must still be the same, and our means essentially the same. Moreover, if you are restricted in your range by poverty, if you cannot buy books and newspapers, for instance, you are but confined to the most significant and vital experiences; you are compelled to deal with the material which yields the most sugar and the most starch. It is life near the bone where it is sweetest. You are defended from being a trifler. No man loses ever on a lower level by magnanimity on a higher. Superfluous wealth can buy superfluities only. Money is not required to buy one necessary of the soul.

I live in the angle of a leaden wall, into whose composition was poured a little alloy of bell-metal. Often, in the repose of my mid-day, there reaches my ears a confused tintinnabulum from without. It is the noise of my contemporaries. My neighbors tell me of their adventures with famous gentlemen and ladies, what notabilities they met at the dinner-table; but I am no more interested in such things than in the contents of the Daily Times. The interest and the conversation are about costume and manners chiefly; but a goose is a goose still, dress it as you will. They tell me of California and Texas, of England and the Indies, of the Hon. Mr.—of Georgia or of Massachusetts, all transient and fleeting phenomena, till I am ready to leap from their court-yard like the Mameluke bey. I delight to come to my bearings—not walk in procession with pomp and parade, in a conspicuous place, but to walk even with the Builder of the universe, if I may—not to live in this restless, nervous, bustling, trivial Nineteenth Century, but stand or sit thoughtfully while it goes by. What are men celebrating? They are all on a committee of arrangements, and hourly expect a speech from somebody. God is only the president of the day, and Webster is his orator. I love to weigh, to settle, to gravitate toward that which most strongly and rightfully attracts me—not hang by the beam of the scale and try to weigh less—not suppose a case, but take the case that is; to travel the only path I can, and that on which no power can resist me. It affords me no satisfaction to commerce to spring an arch before I have got a solid foundation. Let us not play at kittly-benders. There is a solid bottom everywhere. We read that the traveller asked the boy if the swamp before him had a hard bottom. The boy replied that it had. But presently the traveller's horse sank in up to the girths, and he observed to the boy, "I thought you said that this bog had a hard bottom." "So it has," answered the latter, "but you have not got half way to it yet." So it is with the bogs and quicksands of society; but he is an old boy that knows it. Only what is thought, said, or done at a certain rare coincidence is good. I would not be one of those who will foolishly drive a nail into mere lath and plastering; such a deed would keep me awake nights. Give me a hammer, and let me feel for the furring. Do not depend on the putty. Drive a nail home and clinch it so faithfully that you can wake up in the night and think of your work with satisfaction—a work at which you would not be ashamed to invoke the Muse. So will help you God, and so only. Every nail driven should be as another rivet in the machine of the universe, you carrying on the work.

Rather than love, than money, than fame, give me truth. I sat at a table where were rich food and wine in abundance, and obsequious attendance, but sincerity and truth were not; and I went away hungry from the inhospitable board. The hospitality was as cold as the ices. I thought that there was no need of ice to freeze them. They talked to me of the age of the wine and the fame of the vintage; but I thought of an older, a newer, and purer wine, of a more glorious vintage, which they had not got, and could not buy. The style, the house and grounds and "entertainment" pass for nothing with me. I called on the king, but he made me wait in his hall, and conducted like a man incapacitated for hospitality. There was a man in my neighborhood who lived in a hollow tree. His manners were truly regal. I should have done better had I called on him.

How long shall we sit in our porticoes practising idle and musty virtues, which any work would make impertinent? As if one were to begin the day with long-suffering, and hire a man to hoe his potatoes; and in the afternoon go forth to practise Christian meekness and charity with goodness aforethought! Consider the China pride and stagnant self-complacency of mankind. This generation inclines a little to congratulate itself on being the last of an illustrious line; and in Boston and London and Paris and Rome, thinking of its long descent, it speaks of its progress in art and science and literature with satisfaction. There are the Records of the Philosophical Societies, and the public Eulogies of Great Men! It is the good Adam contemplating his own virtue. "Yes, we have done great deeds, and sung divine songs, which shall never die"—that is, as long as we can re-member them. The learned societies and great men of Assyria—where are they? What youthful philosophers and experimentalists we are! There is not one of my readers who has yet lived a whole human life. These may be but the spring months in the life of the race. If we have had the seven-years' itch, we have not seen the seventeen-year locust yet in Concord. We are acquainted with a mere pellicle of the globe on which we live. Most have not delved six feet beneath the surface, nor leaped as many above it. We know not where we are. Beside, we are sound asleep nearly half our time. Yet we esteem ourselves wise, and have an established order on the surface. Truly, we are deep thinkers, we are ambitious spirits! As I stand over the insect crawling amid the pine needles on the forest floor, and endeavoring to conceal itself from my sight, and ask myself why it will cherish those humble thoughts, and hide its head from me who might, perhaps, be its benefactor, and impart to its race some cheering information, I am reminded of the greater Benefactor and Intelligence that stands over me the human insect.

There is an incessant influx of novelty into the world, and yet we tolerate incredible dulness. I need only suggest what kind of sermons are still listened to in the most enlightened countries. There are such words as joy and sorrow, but they are only the burden of a psalm, sung with a nasal twang, while we believe in the ordinary and mean. We think that we can change our clothes only. It is said that the British Empire is very large and respectable, and that the United States are a first-rate power. We do not believe that a tide rises and falls behind every man which can float the British Empire like a chip, if he should ever harbor it in his mind. Who knows what sort of seventeen-year locust will next come out of the ground? The government of the world I live in was not framed, like that of Britain, in after-dinner conversations over the wine.

The life in us is like the water in the river. It may rise this year higher than man has ever known it, and flood the parched uplands; even this may be the eventful year, which will drown out all our muskrats. It was not always dry land where we dwell. I see far inland the banks which the stream anciently washed, before science began to record its freshets. Every one has heard the story which has gone the rounds of New England, of a strong and beautiful bug which came out of the dry leaf of an old table of apple-tree wood, which had stood in a farmer's kitchen for sixty years, first in Connecticut, and afterward in Massachusetts—from an egg deposited in the living tree many years earlier still, as appeared by counting the annual layers beyond it; which was heard gnawing out for several weeks, hatched perchance by the heat of an urn. Who does not feel his faith in a resurrection and immortality strengthened by hearing of this? Who knows what beautiful and winged life, whose egg has been buried for ages under many concentric layers of woodenness in the dead dry life of society, deposited at first in the alburnum of the green and living tree, which has been gradually converted into the semblance of its well-seasoned tomb—heard perchance gnawing out now for years by the astonished family of man, as they sat round the festive board—may unexpectedly come forth from amidst society's most trivial and handselled furniture, to enjoy its perfect summer life at last!

I do not say that John or Jonathan will realize all this; but such is the character of that morrow which mere lapse of time can never make to dawn. The light which puts out our eyes is darkness to us. Only that day dawns to which we are awake. There is more day to dawn. The sun is but a morning star.

CIVIL DISOBEDIENCE

Thoreau's "Civil Disobedience" first appeared in 1849, printed in Elizabeth Peabody's journal *Aesthetic Papers* under the title "Resistance to Civil Government." Its central feature is Thoreau's account of the night he spent in jail for refusing to pay the poll tax. This famous incident has attracted legendary status, but was uneventful and quietly disposed of when someone (unknown to us) paid the tax for him. The theme, however, is crucial to the theme of individual conscience in relation to civil authority, and it formed a piece of the growing mood of protest over slavery.

I heartily accept the motto,—"That government is best which governs least"; and I should like to see it acted up to more rapidly and systematically. Carried out, it finally amounts to this, which also I believe,—"That government is best which governs not at all"; and when men are prepared for it, that will be the kind of government which they will have. Government is at best but an expedient; but most governments are usually, and all governments are some-times, inexpedient. The objections which have been brought against a standing army, and they are many and weighty, and deserve to prevail, may also at last be brought against a standing government. The standing army is only an arm of the standing government. The government itself, which is only the mode which the people have chosen to execute their will, is equally liable to be abused and perverted before the people can act through it. Witness the present Mexican war, the work of comparatively a few individuals using the standing government as their tool; for, in the outset, the people would not have consented to this measure.

This American government—what is it but a tradition, though a recent one, endeavoring to transmit itself unim-paired to posterity, but each instant losing some of its in-tegrity? It has not the vitality and force of a single living man; for a single man can bend it to his will. It is a sort of wooden gun to the people themselves. But it is not the less necessary for this; for the people must have some complicated machinery or other, and hear its din, to satisfy that idea of government which they have. Governments show thus how successfully men can be imposed on, even impose on themselves, for their own advantage. It is excellent, we must all allow. Yet this government never of itself furthered any enterprise, but by the alacrity with which it got out of its way. It does not keep the country free. It does not settle the West. It does not educate. The character inherent in the American people has done all that has been accomplished; and it would have done somewhat more, if the government had not sometimes got in its way. For government is an expedient by which men would fain succeed in letting one another alone; and, as has been said, when it is most expedient, the governed are most let alone by it. Trade and commerce, if they were not made of India rubber, would never manage to bounce over the obstacles which legislators are continually putting in their way; and, if one were to judge these men wholly by the effects of their actions, and not partly by their intentions, they would deserve to be classed and punished with those mischievous persons who put obstructions on the railroads.

But, to speak practically and as a citizen, unlike those who call themselves no-government men, I ask for, not at once no government, but at once a better government. Let every man make known what kind of government would command his respect, and that will be one step toward obtaining it.

After all, the practical reason why, when the power is once in the hands of the people, a majority are permitted, and for a long period continue, to rule, is not because they are most likely to be in the right, nor because this seems fairest to the minority, but because they are physically the strongest. But a government in which the majority rule in all cases cannot be based on justice, even as far as men understand it. Can there not be a government in which majorities do not virtually decide right and wrong, but conscience?—in which majorities decide only those questions to which the rule of expediency is applicable? Must the citizen ever for a moment, or in the least degree, resign his conscience to the legislator? Why has every man a conscience, then? I think that we should be men first, and subjects afterward. It is not desirable to cultivate a respect for the law, so much as for the right. The only obligation which I have a right to assume is to do at any time what I think right. It is truly enough said that a corporation has no conscience; but a corporation of conscientious men is a corporation with a conscience. Law never made men a whit more just; and, by means of their respect for it, even the well-disposed are daily made the agents of injustice. A common and natural result of an undue respect for law is, that you may see a file of soldiers, colonel, captain, corporal, privates, powder-monkeys, and all, marching in admirable order over hill and dale to the wars, against their wills, ay, against their common sense and consciences, which makes it very steep marching indeed, and produces a palpitation of the heart. They have no doubt that it is a damnable business in which they are concerned; they are all peaceably inclined. Now, what are they? Men at all? or small movable forts and magazines, at the service of some unscrupulous man in power? Visit the Navy Yard, and behold a marine, such a man as an American government can make, or such as it can make a man with its black arts—a mere shadow and reminiscence of humanity, a man laid out alive and standing, and already, as one may say, buried under arms with funeral accompaniments, though it may be

> *"Not a drum was heard, not a funeral note,*
> *As his corse to the rampart we hurried;*
> *Not a soldier discharged his farewell shot*
> *O'er the grave where our hero we buried."*

The mass of men serve the state thus, not as men mainly, but as machines, with their bodies. They are the standing army, and the militia, jailers, constables, posse comitatus, etc. In most cases there is no free exercise whatever of the judgment or of the moral sense; but they put themselves on a level with wood and earth and stones; and wooden men can perhaps be manufactured that will serve the purpose as well. Such command no more respect than men of straw or a lump of dirt. They have the same sort of worth only as horses and dogs. Yet such as these even are commonly esteemed good citizens. Others, as most legislators, politicians, lawyers, ministers, and office-holders, serve the state chiefly with their heads; and, as they rarely make any moral distinctions, they are as likely to serve the devil, without intending it, as God. A very few, as heroes, patriots, martyrs, reformers in the great sense, and men, serve the state with their consciences also, and so necessarily resist it for the most part; and they are commonly treated as enemies by it. A wise man will only be useful as a man, and will not submit to be "clay," and "stop a hole to keep the wind away," but leave that office to his dust at least:—

"I am too high-born to be propertied,
To be a secondary at control,
Or useful serving-man and instrument
To any sovereign state throughout the world."

He who gives himself entirely to his fellow-men appears to them useless and selfish; but he who gives himself partially to them is pronounced a benefactor and philanthropist.

How does it become a man to behave toward this American government to-day? I answer, that he cannot without disgrace be associated with it. I cannot for an instant recognize that political organization as my government which is the slave's government also.

All men recognize the right of revolution; that is, the right to refuse allegiance to, and to resist, the government, when its tyranny or its inefficiency are great and unendurable. But almost all say that such is not the case now. But such was the case, they think, in the Revolution of '75. If one were to tell me that this was a bad government because it taxed certain foreign commodities brought to its ports, it is most probable that I should not make an ado about it, for I can do without them. All machines have their friction; and possibly this does enough good to counterbalance the evil. At any rate, it is a great evil to make a stir about it. But when the friction comes to have its machine, and oppression and robbery are organized, I say, let us not have such a machine any longer. In other words, when a sixth of the population of a nation which has undertaken to be the refuge of liberty are slaves, and a whole country is unjustly overrun and conquered by a foreign army, and subjected to military law, I think that it is not too soon for honest men to rebel and revolutionize. What makes this duty the more urgent is the fact that the country so overrun is not our own, but ours is the invading army.

Paley, a common authority with many on moral questions, in his chapter on the "Duty of Submission to Civil Government," resolves all civil obligation into expediency; and he proceeds to say that "so long as the interest of the whole society requires it, that is, so long as the established government cannot be resisted or changed without public inconveniency, it is the will of God that the established government be obeyed, and no longer"—"This principle being admitted, the justice of every particular case of resistance is reduced to a computation of the quantity of the danger and grievance on the one side, and of the probability and expense of redressing it on the other." Of this, he says, every man shall judge for himself. But Paley appears never to have contemplated those cases to which the rule of expediency does not apply, in which a people, as well as an individual, must do justice, cost what it may. If I have unjustly wrested a plank from a drowning man, I must restore it to him though I drown myself. This, according to Paley, would be inconvenient. But he that would save his life, in such a case, shall lose it. This people must cease to hold slaves, and to make war on Mexico, though it cost them their existence as a people.

In their practice, nations agree with Paley; but does any one think that Massachusetts does exactly what is right at the present crisis?

> *"A drab of state, a cloth-o'-silver slut,*
> *To have her train borne up, and her soul trail in the dirt."*

Practically speaking, the opponents to a reform in Massachusetts are not a hundred thousand politicians at the South, but a hundred thousand merchants and farmers here, who are more interested in commerce and agriculture than they are in humanity, and are not prepared to do justice to the slave and to Mexico, cost what it may. I quarrel not with far-off foes, but with those who, near at home, co-operate with, and do the bidding of those far away, and without whom the latter would be harmless. We are accustomed to say, that the mass of men are unprepared; but improvement is slow, because the few are not materially wiser or better than the many. It is not so important that many should be as good as you, as that there be some absolute goodness somewhere; for that will leaven the whole lump. There are thousands who are in opinion opposed to slavery and to the war, who yet in effect do nothing to put an end to them; who, esteeming themselves children of Washington and Franklin, sit down with their hands in their pockets, and say that they know not what to do, and do nothing; who even postpone the question of freedom to the question of free-trade, and quietly read the prices-current along with the latest advices from Mexico, after dinner, and, it may be, fall asleep over them both. What is the price-current of an honest man and patriot to-day? They hesitate, and they regret, and sometimes they petition; but they do nothing in earnest and with effect. They will wait, well disposed, for others to remedy the evil, that they may no longer have it to regret. At most, they give only a cheap vote, and a feeble countenance and Godspeed, to the right, as it goes by them. There are nine hundred and ninety-nine patrons of virtue to one virtuous man; but it is easier to deal with the real possessor of a thing than with the temporary guardian of it.

All voting is a sort of gaming, like checkers or backgammon, with a slight moral tinge to it, a playing with right and wrong, with moral questions; and betting naturally accompanies it. The character of the voters is not staked. I cast my vote, perchance, as I think right; but I am not vitally concerned that that right should prevail. I am willing to leave it to the majority. Its obligation, therefore, never exceeds that of expediency. Even voting for the right is doing nothing for it. It is only expressing to men feebly your desire that it should prevail. A wise man will not leave the right to the mercy of chance, nor wish it to prevail through the power of the majority. There is but little virtue in the action of masses of men. When the majority shall at length vote for the abolition of slavery, it will be because they are indifferent to slavery, or because there is but little slavery left to be abolished by their vote. They will then be the only slaves. Only his vote can hasten the abolition of slavery who asserts his own freedom by his vote.

I hear of a convention to be held at Baltimore, or elsewhere, for the selection of a candidate for the Presidency, made up chiefly of editors, and men who are politicians by profession; but I think, what is it to any independent, intelligent, and respectable man what decision they may come to? Shall we not have the advantage of his wisdom and honesty, nevertheless? Can we not count upon some independent votes? Are there not many individuals in the country who do not attend conventions? But no: I find that the respectable man, so called, has immediately drifted from his position, and despairs of his country, when his country has more reason to despair of him. He forthwith adopts one of the candidates thus selected as the only available one, thus proving that he is himself available for any purposes of the demagogue. His vote is of no more worth than that of any unprincipled foreigner or hireling native, who may have been bought. Oh for a man who is a man, and, as my neighbor says, has a bone in his back which you cannot pass your hand through! Our statistics are at fault: the population has been returned too large. How many men are there to a square thousand miles in this country? Hardly one. Does not America offer any inducement for men to settle here? The American has dwindled into an Odd Fellow—one who may be known by the development of his organ of gregariousness, and a manifest lack of intellect and cheerful self-reliance; whose first and chief concern, on coming into the world, is to see that the almshouses are in good repair; and, before yet he has lawfully donned the virile garb, to collect a fund for the support of the widows and orphans that may be; who, in short ventures to live only by the aid of the Mutual Insurance company, which has promised to bury him decently.

It is not a man's duty, as a matter of course, to devote himself to the eradication of any, even the most enormous wrong; he may still properly have other concerns to engage him; but it is his duty, at least, to wash his hands of it, and, if he gives it no thought longer, not to give it practically his support. If I devote myself to other pursuits and contemplations, I must first see, at least, that I do not pursue them sitting upon another man's shoulders. I must get off him first, that he may pursue his contemplations too. See what gross inconsistency is tolerated. I have heard some of my townsmen say, "I should like to have them order me out to help put down an insurrection of the slaves, or to march to Mexico;—see if I would go"; and yet these very men have each, directly by their allegiance, and so indirectly, at least, by their money, furnished a substitute. The soldier is applauded who refuses to serve in an unjust war by those who do not refuse to sustain the unjust government which makes the war; is applauded by those whose own act and authority he disregards and sets at naught; as if the state were penitent to that degree that it hired one to scourge it while it sinned, but not to that degree that it left off sinning for a moment. Thus, under the name of Order and Civil Government, we are all made at last to pay homage to and support our own meanness. After the first blush of sin comes its indifference; and from immoral it becomes, as it were, unmoral, and not quite unnecessary to that life which we have made.

The broadest and most prevalent error requires the most disinterested virtue to sustain it. The slight reproach to which the virtue of patriotism is commonly liable, the noble are most likely to incur. Those who, while they disapprove of the character and measures of a government, yield to it their allegiance and support are undoubtedly its most conscientious supporters, and so frequently the most serious obstacles to reform. Some are petitioning the State to dissolve the Union, to disregard the requisitions of the President. Why do they not dissolve it themselves—the union between themselves and the State—and refuse to pay their quota into its treasury? Do not they stand in the same relation to the State, that the State does to the Union? And have not the same reasons prevented the State from resisting the Union, which have prevented them from resisting the State?

How can a man be satisfied to entertain an opinion merely, and enjoy it? Is there any enjoyment in it, if his opinion is that he is aggrieved? If you are cheated out of a single dollar by your neighbor, you do not rest satisfied with knowing that you are cheated, or with saying that you are cheated, or even with petitioning him to pay you your due; but you take effectual steps at once to obtain the full amount, and see that you are never cheated again. Action from principle—the perception and the performance of right—changes things and relations; it is essentially revolutionary, and does not consist wholly with anything which was. It not only divides states and churches, it divides families; ay, it divides the individual, separating the diabolical in him from the divine.

Unjust laws exist; shall we be content to obey them, or shall we endeavor to amend them, and obey them until we have succeeded, or shall we transgress them at once? Men generally, under such a government as this, think that they ought to wait until they have persuaded the majority to alter them. They think that, if they should resist, the remedy would be worse than the evil. But it is the fault of the government itself that the remedy is worse than the evil. It makes it worse. Why is it not more apt to anticipate and provide for reform? Why does it not cherish its wise minority? Why does it cry and resist before it is hurt? Why does it not encourage its citizens to be on the alert to point out its faults, and do better than it would have

them? Why does it always crucify Christ, and excommuni-
cate Copernicus and Luther, and pronounce Washington
and Franklin rebels?

One would think, that a deliberate and practical denial
of its authority was the only offence never contemplated by
government; else, why has it not assigned its definite, its
suitable and proportionate, penalty? If a man who has no
property refuses but once to earn nine shillings for the State,
he is put in prison for a period unlimited by any law that I
know, and determined only by the discretion of those who
placed him there; but if he should steal ninety times nine
shillings from the State, he is soon permitted to go at
large again.

If the injustice is part of the necessary friction of the machine of government, let it go, let it go; perchance it will
wear smooth—certainly the machine will wear out. If the
injustice has a spring, or a pulley, or a rope, or a crank, exclusively for itself, then perhaps you may consider whether
the remedy will not be worse than the evil; but if it is of such
a nature that it requires you to be the agent of injustice to
another, then, I say, break the law. Let your life be a counter
friction to stop the machine. What I have to do is to see, at
any rate, that I do not lend myself to the wrong which
I condemn.

As for adopting the ways which the State has provided
for remedying the evil, I know not of such ways. They take
too much time, and a man's life will be gone. I have other
affairs to attend to. I came into this world, not chiefly to
make this a good place to live in, but to live in it, be it good
or bad. A man has not everything to do, but something; and
because he cannot do everything, it is not necessary that he

should do something wrong. It is not my business to be petitioning the Governor or the Legislature any more than it is theirs to petition me; and if they should not hear my petition, what should I do then? But in this case the State has provided no way; its very Constitution is the evil. This may seem to be harsh and stubborn and unconciliatory; but it is to treat with the utmost kindness and consideration the only spirit that can appreciate or deserves it. So is all change for the better, like birth and death which convulse the body.

I do not hesitate to say, that those who call themselves Abolitionists should at once effectually withdraw their support, both in person and property, from the government of Massachusetts, and not wait till they constitute a majority of one, before they suffer the right to prevail through them. I think that it is enough if they have God on their side, without waiting for that other one. Moreover, any man more right than his neighbors constitutes a majority of one already.

I meet this American government, or its representative, the State government, directly, and face to face, once a year—no more—in the person of its tax-gatherer; this is the only mode in which a man situated as I am necessarily meets it; and it then says distinctly, Recognize me; and the simplest, the most effectual, and, in the present posture of affairs, the indispensablest mode of treating with it on this head, of expressing your little satisfaction with and love for it, is to deny it then. My civil neighbor, the tax-gatherer, is the very man I have to deal with—for it is, after all, with men and not with parchment that I quarrel—and he has voluntarily chosen to be an agent of the government. How shall he ever know well what he is and does as an officer of the government, or as a man, until he is obliged to consider whether he shall treat me, his neighbor, for whom he has respect, as a neighbor and well-disposed man, or as a maniac and disturber of the peace, and see if he can get over this obstruction to his neighborliness without a ruder and more impetuous thought or speech corresponding with his action? I know this well, that if one thousand, if one hundred, if ten men whom I could name—if ten honest men only— ay, if one HONEST man, in this State of Massachusetts, ceasing to hold slaves, were actually to withdraw from this copartnership, and be locked up in the county jail therefor, it would be the abolition of slavery in America. For it matters not how small the beginning may seem to be: what is once well done is done forever. But we love better to talk about it: that we say is our mission. Reform keeps many scores of newspapers in its service, but not one man. If my esteemed neighbor, the State's ambassador, who will devote his days to the settlement of the question of human rights in the Council Chamber, instead of being threatened with the prisons of Carolina, were to sit down the prisoner of Massachusetts, that State which is so anxious to foist the sin of slavery upon her sister—though at present she can discover only an act of inhospitality to be the ground of a quarrel with her—the Legislature would not wholly waive the subject the following winter.

Under a government which imprisons any unjustly, the true place for a just man is also a prison. The proper place to-day, the only place which Massachusetts has provided for her freer and less desponding spirits, is in her prisons, to be put out and locked out of the State by her own act, as they have already put themselves out by their principles. It is there that the fugitive slave, and the Mexican prisoner on parole, and the Indian come to plead the wrongs of his race, should find them; on that separate, but more free and honorable ground, where the State places those who are not with her, but against her—the only house in a slave State in which a free man can abide with honor. If any think that their influence would be lost there, and their voices no longer afflict the ear of the State, that they would not be as an enemy within its walls, they do not know by how much truth is stronger than error, nor how much more eloquently and effectively he can combat injustice who has experienced a little in his own person. Cast your whole vote, not a strip of paper merely, but your whole influence. A minority is powerless while it conforms to the majority; it is not even a minority then; but it is irresistible when it clogs by its whole weight. If the alternative is to keep all just men in prison, or give up war and slavery, the State will not hesitate which to choose. If a thousand men were not to pay their tax-bills this year, that would not be a violent and bloody measure, as it would be to pay them, and enable the State to commit violence and shed innocent blood. This is, in fact, the definition of a peaceable revolution, if any such is possible. If the tax-gatherer, or any other public officer, asks me, as one has done, "But what shall I do?" my answer is, "If you really wish to do anything, resign your office." When the subject has refused allegiance, and the officer has resigned his office, then the revolution is accomplished. But even suppose blood should flow. Is there not a sort of blood shed when the conscience is wounded? Through this wound a man's real manhood and immortality flow out, and he bleeds to an everlasting death. I see this blood flowing now.

I have contemplated the imprisonment of the offender, rather than the seizure of his goods—though both will serve the same purpose—because they who assert the purest right, and consequently are most dangerous to a corrupt State, commonly have not spent much time in accumulating property. To such the State renders comparatively small service, and a slight tax is wont to appear exorbitant, particularly if they are obliged to earn it by special labor with their hands. If there were one who lived wholly without the use of money, the State itself would hesitate to demand it of him. But the rich man—not to make any invidious comparison—is always sold to the institution which makes him rich. Absolutely speaking, the more money, the less virtue; for money comes between a man and his objects, and obtains them for him; and it was certainly no great virtue to obtain it. It puts to rest many questions which he would otherwise be taxed to answer; while the only new question which it puts is the hard but superfluous one, how to spend it. Thus his moral ground is taken from under his feet. The opportunities of living are diminished in proportion as what are called the "means" are increased. The best thing a man can do for his culture when he is rich is to endeavor to carry out those schemes which he entertained when he was poor. Christ answered the Herodians according to their condition. "Show me the tribute-money," said he;—and one took a penny out of his pocket;—if you use money which has the image of Caesar on it, and which he has made current and valuable, that is, if you are men of the State, and gladly enjoy the advantages of Caesar's government, then pay him back some of his own when he demands it; "Render therefore to Caesar that which is Caesar's, and to God those things which are God's"—leaving them no wiser than before as to which was which; for they did not wish to know.

When I converse with the freest of my neighbors, I perceive that, whatever they may say about the magnitude and seriousness of the question, and their regard for the public tranquillity, the long and the short of the matter is, that they cannot spare the protection of the existing government, and they dread the consequences to their property and families of disobedience to it. For my own part, I should not like to think that I ever rely on the protection of the State. But, if I deny the authority of the State when it presents its tax-bill, it will soon take and waste all my property, and so harass me and my children without end. This is hard. This makes it impossible for a man to live honestly, and at the same time comfortably in outward respects. It will not be worth the while to accumulate property; that would be sure to go again. You must hire or squat somewhere, and raise but a small crop, and eat that soon. You must live within yourself, and depend upon yourself always tucked up and ready for a start, and not have many affairs. A man may grow rich in Turkey even, if he will be in all respects a good subject of the Turkish government. Confucius said, "If a state is governed by the principles of reason, poverty and misery are subjects of shame; if a state is not governed by the principles of reason, riches and honors are the subjects of shame." No: until I want the protection of Massachusetts to be extended to me in some distant Southern port, where my liberty is endangered, or until I am bent solely on building up an estate at home by peaceful enterprise, I can afford to refuse allegiance to Massachusetts, and her right to my property and life. It costs me less in every sense to incur the penalty of disobedience to the State than it would to obey. I should feel as if I were worth less in that case.

Some years ago, the State met me in behalf of the Church, and commanded me to pay a certain sum toward the support of a clergyman whose preaching my father attended, but never I myself. "Pay," it said, "or be locked up in the jail." I declined to pay. But, unfortunately, another man saw fit to pay it. I did not see why the schoolmaster should be taxed to support the priest, and not the priest the schoolmaster: for I was not the State's schoolmaster, but I supported myself by voluntary subscription. I did not see why the lyceum should not present its tax-bill, and have the State to back its demand, as well as the Church. However, at the request of the selectmen, I condescended to make some such statement as this in writing:—"Know all men by these presents, that I, Henry Thoreau, do not wish to be regarded as a member of any incorporated society which I have not joined." This I gave to the town clerk; and he has it. The State, having thus learned that I did not wish to be regarded as a member of that church, has never made a like demand on me since; though it said that it must adhere to its original presumption that time. If I had known how to name them, I should then have signed off in detail from all the societies which I never signed on to; but I did not know where to find a complete list.

I have paid no poll-tax for six years. I was put into a jail once on this account, for one night; and, as I stood considering the walls of solid stone, two or three feet thick, the door of wood and iron, a foot thick, and the iron grating which strained the light, I could not help being struck with the foolishness of that institution which treated me as if I were mere flesh and blood and bones, to be locked up. I wondered that it should have concluded at length that this was the best use it could put me to, and had never thought to avail itself of my services in some way. I saw that, if there was a wall of stone between me and my townsmen, there was a still more difficult one to climb or break through, before they could get to be as free as I was. I did not for a moment feel confined, and the walls seemed a great waste of stone and mortar. I felt as if I alone of all my townsmen had paid my tax. They plainly did not know how to treat me, but behaved like persons who are underbred. In every threat and in every compliment there was a blunder; for they thought that my chief desire was to stand the other side of that stone wall. I could not but smile to see how industriously they locked the door on my meditations, which followed them out again without let or hindrance, and they were really all that was dangerous. As they could not reach me, they had resolved to punish my body; just as boys, if they cannot come at some person against whom they have a spite, will abuse his dog. I saw that the State was half-witted, that it was timid as a lone woman with her silver spoons, and that it did not know its friends from its foes, and I lost all my remaining respect for it, and pitied it.

Thus the State never intentionally confronts a man's sense, intellectual or moral, but only his body, his senses. It is not armed with superior wit or honesty, but with superior physical strength. I was not born to be forced. I will breathe after my own fashion. Let us see who is the strongest. What force has a multitude? They only can force me who obey a higher law than I. They force me to become like themselves. I do not hear of men being forced to have this way or that by masses of men. What sort of life were that to live? When I meet a government which says to me, "Your money or your life," why should I be in haste to give it my money? It may be in a great strait, and not know what to do: I cannot help that. It must help itself; do as I do. It is not worth the while to snivel about it. I am not responsible for the successful working of the machinery of society. I am not the son of the engineer. I perceive that, when an acorn and a chestnut fall side by side, the one does not remain inert to make way for the other, but both obey their own laws, and spring and grow and flourish as best they can, till one, perchance, overshadows and destroys the other. If a plant cannot live according to its nature, it dies; and so a man.

The night in prison was novel and interesting enough. The prisoners in their shirt-sleeves were enjoying a chat and the evening air in the doorway, when I entered. But the jailer said, "Come, boys, it is time to lock up"; and so they dispersed, and I heard the sound of their steps returning into the hollow apartments. My room-mate was introduced to me by the jailer as "a first-rate fellow and a clever man." When the door was locked, he showed me where to hang my hat, and how he managed matters there. The rooms were whitewashed once a month; and this one, at least, was the whitest, most simply furnished, and probably the neatest apartment in the town. He naturally wanted to know where I came from, and what brought me there; and, when I had told him, I asked him in my turn how he came there, presuming him to be an honest man, of course; and, as the world goes, I believe he was. "Why," said he, "they accuse me of burning a barn; but I never did it." As near as I could discover, he had probably gone to bed in a barn when drunk, and smoked his pipe there; and so a barn was burnt. He had the reputation of being a clever man, had been there some three months waiting for his trial to come on, and would have to wait as much longer; but he was quite domesticated and contented, since he got his board for nothing, and thought that he was well treated.

He occupied one window, and I the other; and I saw that if one stayed there long, his principal business would be to look out the window. I had soon read all the tracts that were left there, and examined where former prisoners had broken out, and where a grate had been sawed off, and heard the history of the various occupants of that room; for I found that even here there was a history and a gossip which never circulated beyond the walls of the jail. Probably this is the only house in the town where verses are composed, which are afterward printed in a circular form, but not published. I was shown quite a long list of verses which were composed by some young men who had been detected in an attempt to escape, who avenged themselves by singing them.

I pumped my fellow-prisoner as dry as I could, for fear I should never see him again; but at length he showed me which was my bed, and left me to blow out the lamp.

It was like travelling into a far country, such as I had never expected to behold, to lie there for one night. It seemed to me that I never had heard the town-clock strike before, nor the evening sounds of the village; for we slept with the windows open, which were inside the grating. It was to see my native village in the light of the Middle Ages, and our Concord was turned into a Rhine stream, and visions of knights and castles passed before me. They were the voices of old burghers that I heard in the streets. I was an involuntary spectator and auditor of whatever was done and said in the kitchen of the adjacent village-inn—a wholly new and rare experience to me. It was a closer view of my native town. I was fairly inside of it. I never had seen its institutions before. This is one of its peculiar institutions; for it is a shire town. I began to comprehend what its inhabitants were about.

In the morning, our breakfasts were put through the hole in the door, in small oblong-square tin pans, made to fit, and holding a pint of chocolate, with brown bread, and an iron spoon. When they called for the vessels again, I was green enough to return what bread I had left; but my comrade seized it, and said that I should lay that up for lunch or dinner. Soon after he was let out to work at haying in a neighboring field, whither he went every day, and would not be back till noon; so he bade me good-day, saying that he doubted if he should see me again.

When I came out of prison—for some one interfered, and paid that tax—I did not perceive that great changes had taken place on the common, such as he observed who went in a youth and emerged a tottering and gray-headed man; and yet a change had to my eyes come over the scene—the town, and State, and country—greater than any that mere time could effect. I saw yet more distinctly the State in which I lived. I saw to what extent the people among whom I lived could be trusted as good neighbors and friends; that their friendship was for summer weather only; that they did not greatly propose to do right; that they were a distinct race from me by their prejudices and superstitions, as the Chinamen and Malays are; that in their sacrifices to humanity, they ran no risks, not even to their property; that after all they were not so noble but they treated the thief as he had treated them, and hoped, by a certain outward observance and a few prayers, and by walking in a particular straight though useless path from time to time, to save their souls. This may be to judge my neighbors harshly; for I believe that many of them are not aware that they have such an institution as the jail in their village.

It was formerly the custom in our village, when a poor debtor came out of jail, for his acquaintances to salute him, looking through their fingers, which were crossed to represent the grating of a jail window, "How do ye do?" My neighbors did not thus salute me, but first looked at me, and then at one another, as if I had returned from a long journey. I was put into jail as I was going to the shoemaker's to get a shoe which was mended. When I was let out the next morning, I proceeded to finish my errand, and, having put on my mended shoe, joined a huckleberry party, who were impatient to put themselves under my conduct; and in half an hour—for the horse was soon tackled—was in the midst of a huckleberry field, on one of our highest hills, two miles off, and then the State was nowhere to be seen.

This is the whole history of "My Prisons."

I have never declined paying the highway tax, because I am as desirous of being a good neighbor as I am of being a bad subject; and as for supporting schools, I am doing my part to educate my fellow-countrymen now. It is for no particular item in the tax-bill that I refuse to pay it. I simply wish to refuse allegiance to the State, to withdraw and stand aloof from it effectually. I do not care to trace the course of my dollar, if I could, till it buys a man or a musket to shoot one with—the dollar is innocent—but I am concerned to trace the effects of my allegiance. In fact, I quietly declare war with the State, after my fashion, though I will still make what use and get what advantage of her I can, as is usual in such cases.

If others pay the tax which is demanded of me, from a sympathy with the State, they do but what they have already done in their own case, or rather they abet injustice to a greater extent than the State requires. If they pay the tax from a mistaken interest in the individual taxed, to save his property, or prevent his going to jail, it is because they have not considered wisely how far they let their private feelings interfere with the public good.

This, then, is my position at present. But one cannot be too much on his guard in such a case, lest his action be biased by obstinacy or an undue regard for the opinions of men. Let him see that he does only what belongs to himself and to the hour.

I think sometimes, Why, this people mean well; they are only ignorant; they would do better if they knew how: why give your neighbors this pain to treat you as they are not inclined to? But I think, again, This is no reason why I should do as they do, or permit others to suffer much greater pain of a different kind. Again, I sometimes say to myself, When many millions of men, without heat, without ill-will, without personal feeling of any kind, demand of you a few shillings only, without the possibility, such is their constitution, of retracting or altering their present demand, and without the possibility, on your side, of appeal to any other millions, why expose yourself to this overwhelming brute force? You do not resist cold and hunger, the winds and the waves, thus obstinately; you quietly submit to a thousand similar necessities. You do not put your head into the fire. But just in proportion as I regard this as not wholly a brute force, but partly a human force, and consider that I have relations to those millions as to so many millions of men, and not of mere brute or inanimate things, I see that appeal is possible, first and instantaneously, from them to the Maker of them, and, secondly, from them to themselves. But, if I put my head deliberately into the fire, there is no appeal to fire or to the Maker of fire, and I have only myself to blame. If I could convince myself that I have any right to be satisfied with men as they are, and to treat them accordingly, and not according, in some respects, to my requisitions and expectations of what they and I ought to be, then, like a good Mussulman and fatalist, I should endeavor to be satisfied with things as they are, and say it is the will of God. And, above all, there is this difference between resisting this and a purely brute or natural force, that I can resist this with some effect; but I cannot expect, like Orpheus, to change the nature of the rocks and trees and beasts.

I do not wish to quarrel with any man or nation. I do not wish to split hairs, to make fine distinctions, or set myself up as better than my neighbors. I seek rather, I may say, even an excuse for conforming to the laws of the land. I am but too ready to conform to them. Indeed, I have reason to suspect myself on this head; and each year, as the tax-gatherer comes round, I find myself disposed to review the acts and position of the general and State governments, and the spirit of the people, to discover a pretext for conformity.

"We must affect our country as our parents,
And if at any time we alienate
Our love or industry from doing it honor,
We must respect effects and teach the soul
Matter of conscience and religion,
And not desire of rule or benefit."

I believe that the State will soon be able to take all my work of this sort out of my hands, and then I shall be no better a patriot than my fellow-countrymen. Seen from a lower point of view, the Constitution, with all its faults, is very good; the law and the courts are very respectable; even this State and this American government are, in many respects, very admirable and rare things, to be thankful for, such as a great many have described them; but seen from a point of view a little higher, they are what I have described them; seen from a higher still, and the highest, who shall say what they are, or that they are worth looking at or thinking of at all?

However, the government does not concern me much, and I shall bestow the fewest possible thoughts on it. It is not many moments that I live under a government, even in this world. If a man is thought-free, fancy-free, imagination-free, that which is *not* never for a long time appearing *to be* to him, unwise rulers or reformers cannot fatally interrupt him.

I know that most men think differently from myself; but those whose lives are by profession devoted to the study of these or kindred subjects, content me as little as any. Statesmen and legislators, standing so completely within the institution, never distinctly and nakedly behold it. They speak of moving society, but have no resting-place without it. They may be men of a certain experience and discrimination, and have no doubt invented ingenious and even useful systems, for which we sincerely thank them; but all their wit and usefulness lie within certain not very wide limits. They are wont to forget that the world is not governed by policy and expediency. Webster never goes behind government, and so cannot speak with authority about it. His words are wisdom to those legislators who contemplate no essential reform in the existing government; but for thinkers, and those who legislate for all time, he never once glances at the subject. I know of those whose serene and wise speculations on this theme would soon reveal the limits of his mind's range and hospitality. Yet, compared with the cheap professions of most reformers, and the still cheaper wisdom and eloquence of politicians in general, his are almost the only sensible and valuable words, and we thank Heaven for him. Comparatively, he is always strong, original, and, above all, practical. Still, his quality is not wisdom, but prudence. The lawyer's truth is not truth, but consistency or a consistent expediency. Truth is always in harmony with herself, and is not concerned chiefly to reveal the justice that may consist with wrong-doing. He well deserves to be called, as he has been called, the Defender of the Constitution. There are really no blows to be given by him but defensive ones. He is not a leader, but a follower. His leaders are the men of '87. "I have never made an effort," he says, "and never propose to make an effort; I have never countenanced an effort, and never mean to countenance an effort, to disturb the arrangement as originally made, by which the various States came into the Union." Still thinking of the sanction which the Constitution gives to slavery, he says, "Because it was a part of the original compact—let it stand." Notwithstanding his special acuteness and ability, he is unable to take a fact out of its merely political relations, and behold it as it lies absolutely to be disposed of by the intellect—what, for instance, it behooves a man to do here in America to-day with regard to slavery, but ventures, or is driven, to make some such desperate answer as the following, while professing to speak absolutely, and as a private man—from which what new and singular code of social duties might be inferred? "The manner," says he, "in which the governments of those States where slavery exists are to regulate it is for their own consideration, under their responsibility to their constituents, to the general laws of propriety, humanity, and justice, and to God. Associations formed elsewhere, springing from a feeling of humanity, or any other cause, have nothing whatever to do with it. They have never received any encouragement from me, and they never will."

They who know of no purer sources of truth, who have traced up its stream no higher, stand, and wisely stand, by the Bible and the Constitution, and drink at it there with reverence and humility; but they who behold where it comes trickling into this lake or that pool, gird up their loins once more, and continue their pilgrimage toward its fountain-head.

No man with a genius for legislation has appeared in America. They are rare in the history of the world. There are orators, politicians, and eloquent men, by the thousand; but the speaker has not yet opened his mouth to speak who is capable of settling the much-vexed questions of the day.

We love eloquence for its own sake, and not for any truth which it may utter, or any heroism it may inspire. Our legislators have not yet learned the comparative value of free-trade and of freedom, of union, and of rectitude, to a nation. They have no genius or talent for comparatively humble questions of taxation and finance, commerce and manufacturers and agriculture. If we were left solely to the wordy wit of legislators in Congress for our guidance, uncorrected by the seasonable experience and the effectual complaints of the people, America would not long retain her rank among the nations. For eighteen hundred years, though perchance I have no right to say it, the New Testament has been written; yet where is the legislator who has wisdom and practical talent enough to avail himself of the light which it sheds on the science of legislation?

The authority of government, even such as I am willing to submit to—for I will cheerfully obey those who know and can do better than I, and in many things even those who neither know nor can do so well—is still an impure one: to be strictly just, it must have the sanction and consent of the governed. It can have no pure right over my person and property but what I concede to it. The progress from an absolute to a limited monarchy, from a limited monarchy to a democracy, is a progress toward a true respect for the individual. Even the Chinese philosopher was wise enough to regard the individual as the basis of the empire. Is a democracy, such as we know it, the last improvement possible in government? Is it not possible to take a step further towards recognizing and organizing the rights of man? There will never be a really free and enlightened State until the State comes to recognize the individual as a higher and independent power, from which all its own power and authority are derived, and treats him accordingly. I please myself with imagining a State at least which can afford to be just to all men, and to treat the individual with respect as a neighbor; which even would not think it inconsistent with its own repose if a few were to live aloof from it, not meddling with it, nor embraced by it, who fulfilled all the duties of neighbors and fellow-men. A State which bore this kind of fruit, and suffered it to drop off as fast as it ripened, would prepare the way for a still more perfect and glorious State, which also I have imagined, but not yet anywhere seen.

III

THE TRANSCENDENTAL HERITAGE

INTRODUCTION TO THE
TRANSCENDENTAL HERITAGE

New England Transcendentalism reached maturity through Emerson, but lost its focus at too young an age, proving to be as short-lived as a mainstream movement as its cousins English Romanticism and High German Idealism before that. But each of these flowerings of perennial hope for envisioning the full potential and nature of the human instrument continues to be held in public consciousness through the consistent influence of the *sophia perennis*, or Perennial Philosophy, and through lesser related movements and the work of special individuals.

The Transcendentalists themselves said that what linked them together was the conviction that all spiritual truths were known intuitively by the innate laws of the mind. An additional and perhaps more significant heritage from this brief New England movement was the general creative expansion of the human mind as the instrument of knowledge and power. As Emerson said in lectures to Harvard undergraduates in 1870, "I hope to invite your attention to the laws of the mind,"[33] and he meant to distract them from their sleep. That he would not be satisfied with his effort merely reflects the range of his ambitions and the infinitude of his subject matter, not to mention Harvard's pragmatic tendencies in the period.

Another major theme among these unique and talented individuals was the refusal to accept any category of final answers to the fundamental questions of human life. A wit once said that a conclusion is just a place where we stop thinking. A human being's primary legacy and responsibility is expressive thought, and to accept a dogma thoughtlessly or to settle prematurely upon a system or explanation of human life is to settle for half. The principle is stated in Emerson's observation of himself as an endless seeker with no past at his back.

Emerson had shown that the human mind was a manifestation of the laws of the universe and by paying close, conscious attention to this mind—that is, by waking to its full nature and potential—we have a chance to penetrate the mysteries of the cosmos to its core reality, while understanding that these mysteries are always just that: mysteries. As he said in "Circles," reality is fluid. But we can still take part in this fluid, dynamic process until we come to see that we and it are identical, and that this great mystery was a greater truth than religious dogmas or momentary scientific fact.

It is useful to remember, in exploring the trails left by Transcendentalism, that these thinkers were essentialists, that philosophical notion developed by Aristotle, stating that essence precedes existence, not the other way round.[34] It gave to Emerson his image of the Over-Soul, or Universal Mind, as an expression of the matrix in which we take our life. As he said, we are in it; it is not in us. In philosophy, it was probably Sartre who expressed the contrasting view as clearly as anyone when he argued that Existentialism was derived from the conviction that existence preceded essence and that human consciousness was merely a by-product or epiphenomenon of evolution. And there, of course, the controversy lies, although the materialists insist smugly that the game is over.

Aristotelian essentialism, on the other hand, argues that a pre-existing essence is the cause of consciousness and gives it a universal nature shared by all sentient beings to one degree or another. As John's gospel voiced the matter, "In the beginning was the Word," "Word" in this case being the Greek *logos,* a universal term for the same essence and conceived of by the Greeks as a faculty of being. Seen philosophically, this spiritual affirmation becomes the source of idealism and the ultimate and lasting strength of the Transcendental movement.

In the 1850s the philosophical idealism of the day was eclipsed in New England, not immediately by Pragmatism, but by the pressures to confront slavery. Even Emerson, dedicated as he was to the solitary quest, was swept up and in 1851 delivered his famous Fugitive Slave Law address, marking an end to his practice as a detached scholar. In effect, moral and ethical issues arose to demand action, and the Transcendentalists rose as one to the challenge.

Following the Civil War, one effect of which was to shatter the idealist dream in the national bloodbath, Transcendentalism faded from philosophy to be replaced finally by the new pragmatism. The new philosophy was generated by the work of William James, Charles Peirce, and John Dewey. Like Transcendentalism, the new thought was as varied as there were so-called Pragmatists, but its basic principles were its positive nature, without being necessarily idealist; its theory of signs but not of correspondences; and its focus on specific moral problems, absent a concern with the ultimate truth of reality, the nature of which was regarded as out-of-bounds. The philosophy was "pragmatic" in the sense that if a given belief had a positive effect on a person's life, then it was valid, and it did not so much matter if it couldn't be proved ultimately true or not. The proof, in other words, was in the proverbial pudding.

After 1865, with philosophy taking a different course and Darwinian evolution dominating science, what remained of Transcendentalism was thrust into the hands of religious zealots, poets, and radical thinkers of all stripes. Among the poets, Walt Whitman and, to some extent, Emily Dickinson in the late nineteenth century and Hart Crane, Wallace Stevens, and Robert Frost in the twentieth are not alone but are the central candidates for carrying on the tradition of individual seekers.

MOVEMENTS AND INSTITUTIONS

The Transcendentalists' overlapping interests in all things spiritual, in the potential of the human mind, and in the primacy of nature had a profound influence on a series of movements and institutions that evolved during the nineteenth century and beyond. In particular, Emerson's articulation of the Over-Soul and his intuitions of Universal Mind attracted the attention not only of religious reformers but also of scientific, environmental, and philosophic innovators.

Emerson's *Nature* and Thoreau's *Walden* were two texts that inspired budding naturalists and stimulated the founding of the environmental movement in America. Figures such as John Muir and John Burroughs drew from these texts for their own early work in conservation. And, as mentioned earlier, the environmental movement officially dates itself to the day, July 4, 1845, when Henry Thoreau moved into his cabin at Walden Pond.

Among the spiritual enthusiasts were those practitioners and observers of psychic phenomena, including mesmerism, séances, transmigration of souls, and physical mediumship, all of which gained popular audiences and adherents throughout the 1800s. For the most part, however, these were minor, fleeting interests. Among the more influential and lasting investigators interested in the powers of the human mind were figures such as Mary Baker Eddy (1821–1910), founder of Christian Science; Phineas Quimby (1802–1866), one of the founders of the New Thought movement; and, later, Ernest Holmes (1887–1960), founder of Religious Science. All of these movements combined scientific investigation and physical healing with religious belief in one form or another and sought both to explain and to put into practice the new knowledge arising from the field of psychology then being formulated by William James at Harvard College.

Part of the Tarcher/Penguin series that includes this book is *The Essential Ernest Holmes,* a collection of essays and excerpts from longer works written by the religious thinker. Among them are pieces setting out the principles behind Religious Science. Central to these is the essential unity of all experience. As Holmes said, everything could be reconciled into one "Thing," and this "Thing," also named "Itself," was eternal, fully present, and totally indefinable. What gave his beliefs credibility, in terms the Transcendentalists would have admired, was his conviction that this teaching would remain "forever open at the top"—that is, that new laws and new perceptions would continue to be revealed.[35] His was not a fixed or static vision.

The distinctive characteristic of Religious Science as a hereditary offshoot of New England Transcendentalism is that the original impulse, although philosophical in nature, took form as a religious movement of very broad, universal application. Founded by Holmes in California, the Church of Religious Science has meetings and study groups in more than thirty-six states and fifteen foreign countries. What connects this movement to Emersonian thought is that Holmes, like Emerson before him, emerged from orthodox Christianity into a more universal spiritual understanding of human nature and the universe, and although the teachings of Jesus remain pivotal, the central emphasis is on the infinite possibilities of the Universal Mind accessible to all individuals, regardless of religious persuasion.

Over the years, Religious Science has proven itself a legitimate path of religious and spiritual experience. But it must be said that the landscape is also littered with failed and fringe movements that actively recruit the vulnerable and unwary. In these heady days of the New Age, cults, and gurus from both Eastern and Western esoteric traditions, the sincere seeker is confronted with a dizzying supermarket of attractions promising immortality, salvation, and benefits of all kinds, including material wealth and well-being. Finding a legitimate path to follow requires discrimination and consistent effort, but both these assets are part of any real spiritual exploration.

Throughout much of the twentieth century, the knowledge revealed in the nineteenth concerning the human mind was seized upon by what the writer Colin Wilson has called "rogue messiahs," those who exploit genuine advances in knowledge to take advantage of and profit from the unsuspecting and the gullible. Perhaps the most serious of these charlatans are those who offer for a price to reveal how the human mind can change and control reality. When Emerson, for example, made the statement that we are what we think about all day, he meant, naturally, that what takes place in our minds determines in no small measure who we are. It is a matter of attitude and character, not manipulation of the nature of reality.

The Transcendentalists understood that the truth of reality was the same as the ground state of the universe and not a quality that can be changed by a shift in thinking. It is a characteristic of postmodernism to think of shifting perceptions of reality, making reality something subject to opinion. And when those who are genuinely seeking to understand the nature of reality find themselves on these shifting fault lines, they are vulnerable to those with easy answers and sellers of self-esteem.

Once seekers find themselves drawn to serious spiritual inquiry and experience, a whole world of possibility opens before them. One of the great temptations is the shadowy world of psychic phenomena and what William James cataloged so well in *The Varieties of Religious Experience.* James was justifiably cautious about many of these phenomena, and Emerson, too, warned of excesses. In his late essay "Demonology," he stated this principle: "The history of man is a series of conspiracies to win from Nature some advantage without paying for it. It is curious to see what grand powers we have a hint of and are mad to grasp, yet how slow Heaven is to trust us with such edge-tools."

SOLITARY VOICES

Although the religious and scientific aspects of Transcendentalism created movements and institutions, the literary and poetic heritage of Transcendentalism fell to the poets and writers following the Civil War. Their attraction to the thinking of the founders coalesced around the celebration of the imagination and trust in the intuitive powers of the mind to perceive the world in new ways and to penetrate to the nature of what it means to be human.

WALT WHITMAN (1819–1892)

The first significant heir to the riches of Transcendentalism was Walt Whitman. Although roughly contemporary to Emerson and Thoreau, Whitman lived in New York and in temperament as well as style might as well have been from another world and time. In many ways, not the least of which was his dynamic universal voice, he was the American Homer, cataloging the life, events, and character of the times in their fullest, most graphic terms. What makes him an heir to the Transcendentalists was his sense of the expanded self, the rich, mysterious, inclusive unity of humanity, expressed as Emersonian infinitude. In effect, *Leaves of Grass* would not have been possible without the essays of Emerson, but it was, at the same time, more sweeping, grand, and experimental than anything Emerson would have imagined.

Whitman's flowing pages, his leaves, embrace both nature and human experience as a unity as they explore the essence of a world spirit indicative of Emerson's Over-Soul:

> *And I know that the spirit of God is the eldest brother*
> *of my own,*
> *And that all the men ever born are also my brothers . . . and*
> *the women my sisters and lovers,*
> *And that a kelson of the creation is love;*
> *And limitless are leaves stiff or drooping in the fields,*
> *And brown ants in the little wells beneath them,*

*And mossy scabs of the wormfence, and heaped stones, and
    elder and mullen and pokeweed.*

*A child said, What is the grass? fetching it to me with
    full hands;*
*How could I answer the child? . . . I do not know what it is
    any more than he.*
*I guess it must be the flag of my disposition, out of hopeful
    green stuff woven.*

Or I guess it is the handkerchief of the Lord,
A scented gift and remembrancer designedly dropped,
*Bearing the owner's name someway in the corners, that we
    may see and remark, and say Whose?*

*Or I guess the grass is itself a child . . . the produced babe of
    the vegetation.*

Or I guess it is a uniform hieroglyphic,
*And it means, Sprouting alike in broad zones and
    narrow zones,*
Growing among black folks as among white,
*Kanuck, Tuckahoe, Congressman, Cuff, I give them the
    same, I receive them the same.*

This inclusiveness and seemingly effortless style in moving so
easily between the inner and outer worlds in the direction of
human freedom and power is what must have impressed Emerson
so much and prompted his now famous letter of July 1855, de-
claring, "I greet you at the beginning of a great career." Compared
to the more reserved rhetoric of the Boston Brahmins, Whitman

must have struck Emerson like a tidal wave of raw feeling and experience. Certainly nothing like this had ever crossed his threshold, and his enthusiasm, no matter how much he later expressed reservations about some of the more explicit sexual content, was the mark of an honest and courageous reader. It is difficult to imagine what it must have been like to be the first reader of *Leaves of Grass*.

The question occasionally arises, what is Transcendental about Whitman? The answer depends, of course, on the definition of Transcendentalism one chooses at the outset. In our case, where the term has been taken to reflect a vision of unity, particularly of reason and feeling, and second, to celebrate the intuitive powers of the human mind, Whitman proves to be essential. The poems of *Leaves* fuse reason and feeling into a poetic reality in which the poet and America become the active, dynamic, living creation of the intuitive imagination. The nation and the human being are one and the same, male/female, native/foreigner, mind/body, past/future, all fused into a raucous, sublime, celebratory present.

Even Whitman's prose reflects this fusion. Take this, from the Preface to the 1855 edition of *Leaves of Grass*:

The known universe has one complete lover and that is the greatest poet. He consumes an eternal passion and is indifferent which chance happens and which possible contingency of fortune or misfortune and persuades daily and hourly his delicious pay. What balks or breaks others is fuel for his burning progress to contact and amorous joy. Other proportions of the reception of pleasure dwindle to nothing to his proportions. All expected from heaven or from the highest he is rapport with in the sight of the daybreak or a

scene of the winter woods or the presence of children playing or with his arm round the neck of a man or woman. His
love above all love has leisure and expanse . . . .he leaves
room ahead of himself.

EMILY DICKINSON (1830–1886)

Emily Dickinson was born on December 10, 1830, in Amherst,
Massachusetts, where she remained the rest of her secluded life,
leaving for only a brief stay of one year to attend the Mount
Holyoke Female Seminary in nearby South Hadley. In her lifetime,
living mostly in her room, she wrote nearly 1,800 poems, only six
or seven of which were published while she lived. She died on
May 15, 1886, aged fifty-five, of Bright's disease, a kidney disease
akin to nephritis.

It is hardly commonplace to consider Emily Dickinson an heir
to the Transcendental sensibility. Perhaps she is a distant cousin.
Living as she did in Amherst, far from the influence of Boston and
Harvard, and raised as she was in the Trinitarian tradition (her father was an orthodox Calvinist), Emily had little firsthand contact
with religious reform, and it was also likely that her reclusive nature kept her from church attendance, rather than any serious objection to her tradition.

But what draws her closer to the Transcendentalists are devotion to the examined life and profound mysticism, both exemplified by a consistent attraction to the deepest mysteries of existence
and being. Her poetry was a testimony to her inner life and a
reaching out through poetry to express what could not, ultimately,
be expressed any other way. As a result, her solitary life was both
a choice and a necessity. Unlike Emerson, who thrived as a pub-

lic figure but retired to his study for renewal and inspiration, Dickinson's seclusion was the only way she could commune with the infinite, not just as inspiration but as reality itself.

Here, for example, are two poems that qualify Dickinson for inclusion in the Transcendental circle, if she had been interested in taking her place there.

Some keep the Sabbath going to Church—
I keep it, staying at Home—
With a Bobolink for a Chorister—
And an Orchard, for a Dome—

Some keep the Sabbath in Surplice—
I just wear my Wings—
And instead of tolling the Bell, for Church,
Our little Sexton—sings.

God preaches, a noted Clergyman—
And the sermon is never long,
So instead of getting to Heaven, at last—
I'm going, all along.

Forever—is composed of Nows—
'Tis not a different time—
Except for Infiniteness—
And Latitude of Home—

From this—experienced Here—
Remove the Dates—to These—
Let Months dissolve in further Months—
And Years—exhale in Years—

Without Debate—or Pause—
Or Celebrated Days
No different Our Years would be
From Anno Domini's—

One of the characteristics of the examined life is its intense reliance on knowledge as opposed to faith. It is axiomatic that the
examined life accepts uncertainty and the mystery of the unknown.
Faith removes mystery and replaces it with a system of belief. It was
characteristic of the Transcendentalists that they rejected systems
and thus rejected traditional faith as well.

In Dickinson's case, religious faith was a sometime thing, varying during her life and in her poetry from doubt to assurance, but
never to denial. Her poems encompassed the trials of life, the mysteries of death, and the hopes of immortality. Her poetic images
of the soul contained all the states of existence and were recurring
and familiar symbols in the body of her work. Lines such as "The
soul should always stand ajar," "The soul selects her own society,"
and "Narcotics cannot still the Tooth / that nibbles at the soul"
draw our attention to the inner life and the soul's awakening,
which was a constant theme among the Transcendentalists.

Poem number 822 of the Dickinson canon is, to this reader, the
most transcendental and evocative of the examined life. Its central
image in stanza 2, the "experience between" leading to the "profound experiment" to which the flesh is heir, places Dickinson
squarely in the Emersonian tradition at its most esoteric.

This consciousness that is aware
Of Neighbors and the Sun
Will be the one aware of Death
And that itself alone

Is traversing the interval
Experience between
And most profound experiment
Appointed unto Men—

How adequate unto itself
Its properties shall be
Itself unto itself and none
Shall make discovery

Adventure most unto itself
The Soul condemned to be—
Attended by a single Hound
Its own identity.

Intensely conscious human beings, like Emily Dickinson, live in an interval, a world in between. It is Plato's *metaxi*, the in-between space/time where the human and divine intersect, drawn by *eros*, the passion of the desire to know, met there by divine grace. It is neither here nor there, but is in a gap between and, as Dickinson so clearly says, is an adventure most unto itself. The soul, that different entity, which simply is, accompanied obediently by this consciousness, undertakes the quest as best it can, wary and uncertain of the destination.

WALLACE STEVENS (1879–1955)

Transcendentalism asks and then answers the existential question, Is the examined life necessary? To quote a line from the great American poet Wallace Stevens, "I accept what it means to be in the difficulty of what it is to be."[36] Stevens lived a dual life, writing poetry starting in 1915 and, after gaining a law degree, working in the insurance business, rising to vice president of Hartford Accident and Indemnity. Most of his fellow workers had no idea that their "Wally" wrote poems.

The particular poem by Stevens that speaks directly to his Transcendental roots is *Notes Toward a Supreme Fiction* (1942), a poem in which Stevens explored his notions of reality, which in turn revealed his notions of poetry as the map of the ground of being. Reality for Stevens can only be described or discerned by the emanations of the creative mind. The scientific mind can, of course, also be creative, and at its best moments it is. But the poetic mind allows a broader range of expression, formulating in metaphor the various resemblances inherent in the quest.

The question is, why select something called a "supreme fiction" as an image of the ground of being we are seeking? Aren't we looking for the truth of reality? In what way is the truth a "fiction"? Is there a connection between Stevens's "supreme fiction" and the truth of reality sought by Emerson, Thoreau, and Whitman? The answer lies partly in the nature of modernity and partly in the creative process, that mysterious place which is neither totally within the scope of human consciousness nor entirely foreign to it.

As we saw in the work of Whitman and Dickinson, the poetic imagination takes its vitality from faculties of consciousness, from reason's powers of discrimination and feeling's depth of perception. The unknown element is what we now call the unconscious, that realm of influence, imagery, and archetype that operates beyond conscious awareness and informs the mystery of existence. To deny the deep recesses of the unconscious or to put a strictly Freudian cast upon it simply ignores the extraordinary output of human creativity that we have fortunately been able to record and to preserve.

Stevens's notion of a "supreme fiction" establishes a resemblance between poetic imagery and the truth sought for, because the former describes the nature of the creative imagination in the quest. As conscious human beings, we cannot approach this quest except through the medium of that creative power arising within us. What religion calls revelation is the assertion that the existence and nature of the Absolute does not emerge from this creative force but comes directly from the Word of God. What poets call revelation comes instead from their creative imaginations and is what Stevens chose to call in this instance a supreme fiction. It is a matter of choosing a source.

In addition, the fiction thus conceived is "supreme" because it is transcendental. It creates a world in which we speak of the transcendent "as if" it were real, which of course, it may turn out to be. All we can know, however, is that the world of "as if" is a fictive enhancement of an intuition of a reality. Further than that we cannot go. That limit represents the boundaries of the quest. In the human realm, there are limits, even while consciousness is infinite. So, with that caution, we enter the world of the poem *Notes Toward a Supreme Fiction*.

By the early 1940s, with America at war and with Stevens himself walking to and from his work as a lawyer at the insurance company, his measured steps along the sidewalks of Hartford, Connecticut, set the rhythms for his verse and together with his seeker's heart framed the images that would make the poem his reality, to somehow fuse the profane with the sacred in measured beats and exotic metaphors. In *Notes* he was concerned with creating a new paradigm of the ground, casting out the dead myths of his culture in favor of a new vision. *Notes* would end by being one of his greatest efforts at imagining the transcendent in unprecedented flights of language.

Notes is divided into three large sections, each creating the conditions and imagery necessary to envision a new paradigm of the examined life. Part I, "It Must Be Abstract," sets in motion the concept of the *idea* of the ground of being as the first step. We are not, in other words, starting with a literal ground, but we are also not looking for a vision that is the result of what Stevens calls the "inventing mind."

Stevens was a true seeker, that much is evident from the complete record of his work, begun in the midst of World War I, bursting forth through the '30s and then coming to fruition in the Second World War. He knew the experience of a radical awakening, not just of poetic power but also of philosophical perception and insight. The theme affirms his Transcendental roots.

> *Perhaps there are moments of awakening,*
> *Extreme, fortuitous, personal, in which*
>
> *We more than awaken, sit on the edge of sleep,*
> *As on an elevation, and behold*
> *The academies like structures in a mist.*
> (I, vii, 17–21)

Moving beyond the ideologies of received traditions (the academies), he follows Emerson and Thoreau in seeking to rise above the Past, yet reaching back for the nature of the first idea, to return to a new beginning using the power of creative imagination—again, not through the artifice of invention, but through the deepest resources of the *nous,* an intuitive, universal well-spring of imagination. He is looking for what he calls "balances," not those "we achieve but balances that happen" (I, vii, 15). As he uses the term, this balance is achieved through grace.

Philosophy and creative imagination have not always been on friendly terms, particularly in the Positivist twentieth century, but a proper recognition of the power of creative imagination has historically been an accepted frontier of philosophical investigation. Two sorts have always been in evidence: the fanciful outpourings of spontaneous thought and a more measured creativity prompted by explorations in a chosen direction. In *Notes,* Stevens is the conscious explorer, seeking to define a new order of being by throwing off the limitations of accumulated myth and ideology.

We know, if we are at all watchful, that we live most of our lives on shifting ground, amid a constant quaking within which we are hopeful of finding Emerson's place to stand. In Part II of *Notes,* entitled "It Must Change," Stevens creates a series of vivid images of our struggle on this shifting ground. His created world is full of brilliant colors, redolent odors, changing shapes, and booming bees, in effect "inconstant objects of inconstant cause" (II, i, 11). We seek stability, but first we must understand that the shifting scene repeats itself ad nauseam and will not become still of itself.

> *It means the distaste we feel for this withered scene*
> *Is that it has not changed enough. It remains.*
> *It is a repetition.*
> (II, i, 15–17)

What is needed in this shifting scene is inner transformation. Poets for the most part create what Stevens calls a fictive covering which "weaves always glistening from the heart and mind" (II, viii, 21). This casual shifting of ground asks for more.

> *The freshness of transformation is*
> *The freshness of a world. It is our own,*

It is ourselves, the freshness of ourselves,
And that necessity and that presentation
Are rubbings of a glass in which we peer.
(II, x, 15–18)

Reflection is both deflected image and mental discipline. We are caught in the paradox of having to live amid shifting images while seeking some still point to use as a reference for our seeking. It is fitting, for example, that Henry Thoreau was a surveyor, triangulating his territory as he sought to understand its secrets. The eye fixed to the transit is for that moment the still point, the point of observation, just as the poet's eye fixes the moving world in order to accomplish the longed-for transformation. The eye, as Emerson pointed out, is nature's first circle, its first whole. It is the circle that creates the horizon line.

In Part III, "It Must Give Pleasure," Stevens begins what he calls "the difficultest rigor" in order to catch in the "irrational moment its unreasoning" (III, i, 14–15). It is an affirmation through negation. It is in this last section that Stevens becomes most lyrical in his transcendental quest. It is an outburst of feeling at the fearful outer edges of perception. Once again, we are reminded of Emerson's glimpse of the edge: "I am glad to the brink of fear." It is a sublime experience in the flush of poetic revelation. At the heart of it is the perception of a new order.

To discover an order as of
A season, to discover summer and know it,

To discover winter and know it well, to find,
Not to impose, not to have reasoned at all,
Out of nothing to have come on major weather,

It is possible, possible, possible. It must
Be possible. It must be that in time
The real will from its crude compoundings come,
Seeming, at first, a beast disgorged, unlike,
Warmed by a desperate milk. To find the real,
To be stripped of every fiction except one,

The fiction of an absolute—Angel,
Be silent in your luminous cloud and hear
The luminous melody of proper sound.
(III, vii, 8–21)

We see Stevens here veering off the "real" at the last moment, unable or unwilling to stay with an abstract Absolute. Suddenly, the angel/goddess breaks through the opaque world into vivid transparency, a poetic image from the poet who is seeking real being. But we feel nonetheless his affirmation of what has to be possible in the end. Stevens the poet knits the dualities of the world together into an image of the whole, but as he says, "It is a war that never ends." The efforts continue always, just as the quest goes on.

The poetry discussed above is complex, but is not meant to be a celebration of complexity or obscurity for their own sakes. That Dickinson and Stevens are difficult has more to do with their vision and purpose than a particular taste for elitism or loftiness. Eliot had it right when he talked about language deteriorating at crucial points into imprecision, of wanting so much to say what cannot concretely be said, or said at all, that the poet's use of language becomes compact and elusive. But mystics of all kinds have a reputation for obscurity because they dwell in distant lands and report back to us mere mortals in symbols that shimmer in fading light and echo the sounds of distant calls.

THE NATURE WRITERS

"Nature prefers to hide," said the pre-Socratic Heraclitus, who knew what he was talking about. As we saw in the era of Emerson and Thoreau, it is nature that still remains central to the heritage of the Transcendentalists. Nature in all her complexity is the place where the secrets of existence and being are to be found, not in human cities and human structures and machines. Nature unadorned, unaltered, when it can be found and properly studied, is where to seek our reports of the truth of reality, and it is among the writers and chroniclers of nature, from the macrocosms to the microcosms that we search these days.

Voices such as Loren Eiseley's and Annie Dillard's have stood out in the chorus of nature writers of recent vintage who have kept the Transcendental vision alive. Along with their admirers and imitators, they have gone out alone into the wilderness and watched and listened and then recorded faithfully what they witnessed there. It is a tradition beginning with Thoreau and followed by John Muir, John Burroughs, and others and culminating in the present day with the environmentalism of activists such as Terry Tempest Williams and Julia Butterfly Hill.[37]

LOREN EISELEY (1907–1977)

The path of Transcendentalism in the twentieth century was trod not only by poets. It was the age of science, after all, not poetry; and the forces of materialism and scientism were dominant. A few serious thinkers, however, kept alive the broad themes of a more expansive, less narrow vision, and one such scientist was Loren

Eiseley, anthropologist, writer, teacher, and naturalist. Eiseley combined a solid grasp of scientific empiricism with a profound trust in his intuitive insight into the nature and meaning of things. That combination was reflected in more than ten books as well as numerous lectures and essay collections over a long and distinguished career.

Eiseley's debt to Emerson and Thoreau is clear in his work, and it is doubtful that he would have emerged as a major writer and influential thinker without their influence. Here, for example, is a passage from *The Invisible Pyramid* (1970) in which he reflects upon human destiny:

> The story of the great saviors, whether Chinese, Indian, Greek, or Judaic, is the story of man in the process of enlightening himself, not simply by tools, but through the slow inward growth of the mind that made and may yet master them through knowledge of itself. "The poet, like the lightning rod," Emerson once stated, "must reach from a point nearer the sky than all surrounding objects down to the earth, and into the dark, wet soil, or neither is of use." Today that effort is demanded not only of the poet. In the age of space it is demanded of all of us. Without it there can be no survival of mankind, for man himself must be his last magician. He must seek his own way home.[38]

Eiseley was attracted to correspondences like the poet and the lightning rod because he saw the accuracy in them, the profound connection between the mind and nature. And it was in his small book *The Mind As Nature* that he set down his most valuable observations of that connection.

Although Eiseley worked within the confines of an academic institution all his professional life, he had the released time of research in the wilderness and among native peoples and strange cultures. He brought that experience back to the classroom with him and gave his students the benefit of his wisdom. He knew the tension of being part of a university structure and yet was able to be free of it as well. In *The Mind As Nature,* Eiseley confronted the problem of the questing mind held within the bounds of an institution.

Now we as teachers, responsible to society, will appreciate that certain of these ancient institutions by which men live, are, however, involved with human imperfection, the supporting bones of the societal body. Without them, without a certain degree of conformity and habit, society would literally cease to exist. The problem lies in sustaining the airy flight of the superior intellect above the necessary ruts it is forced to travel. As Thoreau comments, the heel of the true author wears out no road. "A thinker's weight is in his thought, not in his tread."[39]

Finally, however, for Eiseley, the search for the truth of reality is found only in solitary exploration in the wilderness of nature. He ends his small book with this reminiscence:

In Bimini, on the old Spanish Main, a black girl once said to me: "Those as hunts treasure must go alone, at night, and when they find it they have to leave a little of their blood behind them."

I have never heard a fine, cleaner estimate of the price of wisdom. I wrote it down at once under a sea lamp, like the belated pirate I was, for the girl had given me unknowingly the latitude and longitude of a treasure—a treasure more valuable than all the aptitude tests of this age.[40]

ANNIE DILLARD (B. 1945)

Annie Dillard is a gifted, influential, and transcendental voice for our own time, leafing through the documents of the earth for hints of the ground of being. Her Pulitzer Prize–winning *Pilgrim at Tinker Creek* (1974) alone would give her a prominent place among these names, and her book ends with a celebration of Emerson and Stevens's angel of the Absolute. She reminds us that human life is a great privilege, particularly if we are awake enough to be conscious witnesses. The immortal gods, despite their power and glory, do not experience life, and therefore cannot aspire or understand transformation or the transcendent. We, on the other hand, have the world to devour and to transform.

One such collective transformation occurred in 1969 when, for the first time, humanity saw a photograph of the earth taken from the moon. It was the size of an apple, floating in the void of space. It is remarkable that Emerson, more than a century earlier, had a dream of the same image. Dillard realized it, too, and reported his journal entry at the close of *Tinker Creek*.

> Emerson saw it. "I dreamed that I floated at will in the great Ether, and I saw this world floating also not far off, but diminished to the size of an apple. Then an angel took it in his hand and brought it to me and said, 'This thou must eat.' And I ate the world." All of it. All of it intricate, speckled, gnawed, fringed, and free.[41]

As we learned in Emerson's essay "Circles," "our life is an apprenticeship to the truth, that around every circle another can be drawn; that there is no end in nature, but every end is a beginning; that there is always another dawn risen on mid-noon, and under every deep a lower deep opens." We come full circle, then, to an observation made by the great American writer E. L. Doctorow, in his book *Reporting the Universe*, the first chapter of which is entitled "Emerson."

We shall end where Doctorow begins. First, a quote from Emerson's essay "Goethe, or the Writer":

The Writer . . . believes all that can be thought can be written. . . . In his eyes a man is the faculty of reporting, and the universe is the possibility of being reported.

Then, from Doctorow:

These lines come of an earlier time in American letters, when the word universe did not invoke thoughts of the Big Bang but only meant . . . everything.

As the poet, essayist, Transcendentalist, and lapsed preacher Ralph Waldo Emerson conceives it, we are not about a fixed discoverable universe, but one constantly adjusting to the human inquiry. The universe as the possibility of being reported suggests endless ascription, infinite surprise.

Finally, the faculty of reporting and the possibility of being reported comprise the phenomenal crisis of human consciousness—which Emerson views with fascination as our great glory.[42]

Whether or not we rise to that glory is a choice, not an accident of fate or heredity. Choosing affirmation rather than rejection takes us out of ignorance into freedom, that sometimes-frightening place where the well-worn paths of others fade and we have to strike out on our own. That choice is Essential Transcendentalism.

NOTES

1. Aldous Huxley, *The Perennial Philosophy* (New York; Harper & Row, 1970), p. vii.
2. Thomas Taylor, *The Complete Works of Plato* (London, 1803), p. lxx.
3. Robert D. Richardson, Jr., *Emerson: The Mind on Fire* (Berkeley: University of California Press, 1995), pp. 30–31.
4. Ibid., p. 31.
5. Wordsworth material taken from the Internet: www.everypoet.com/archive/poetry/William_Wordsworth/william_wordsworth_331.htm.
6. Richardson, p. 146.
7. James Freeman Clarke, *Autobiography, Diary, and Correspondence*, edited by Edward Everett Hale (Boston: Houghton Mifflin, 1891), p. 38.
8. Richardson, p. 166.
9. *Transcendentalism,* edited by Joel Myerson (New York and London: Oxford University Press, 2000), p. 92.
10. Richardson, p. 166.
11. Ralph Waldo Emerson, "Prospects," in *Nature.*
12. Octavius Frothingham, *Transcendentalism in New England* (New York, 1876; New York: Harper Torchbooks, 1959), p. 250.
13. Richard G. Geldard, *God in Concord* (Burdett, N.Y.: Larson Publications, 1999), p. 112.
14. Emerson, *Nature.*
15. *The Journals of Bronson Alcott,* edited by Odell Shepard (Boston: Little, Brown, 1938).
16. *The Journals and Miscellaneous Notebooks of Ralph Waldo Emerson,* edited by William H. Gilman, Ralph H. Orth, et al., 16 vols. (Cambridge: Harvard University Press, 1982), VII, p. 342. Hereafter JMN.
17. Emerson, "The Senses and the Soul," in *Dial,* vol. 3.
18. William Kilpatrick, *Heinrich Pestalozzi: The Education of Man—Aphorisms* (New York: Philosophical Library, 1951).
19. Eric Voegelin, *In Search of Order* (Baton Rouge: Louisiana State University Press, 1987), p. 15.

20. JMN IV, p. 273.

21. JMN IV, p. 87.

22. Laurence Buell, *Emerson* (Cambridge: Harvard University Press, 2003), p. 123.

23. *Emerson in His Journals,* edited by Joel Porte (Cambridge: Harvard University Press, 1982), p. 413.

24. Research into the records of the Ossoli family suggests that the couple did in fact marry prior to the birth of their son. It is logical, given the times, although the union may well have been a civil one.

25. Richardson, p. 483.

26. *The Journals of Henry David Thoreau,* vol. 1 (Salt Lake City: Peregrine Smith Books, 1984), p. 3. Hereafter JHDT.

27. JHDT, vol. 1, pp. 53–54.

28. JHDT, vol. 1, p. 9.

29. According to the Ecology Hall of Fame in its published "Environmental Timeline," the starting point for the environmental movement in America is dated from July 4, 1845, when Thoreau first moved into his cabin.

30. The book was published on August 9, 1854, by Ticknor and Company of Boston in an edition of 2,000 copies. The book sold slowly, going out of print in 1859. From then until 1862, when Thoreau died, is the only time it has been out of print. Since then, well over 200 different editions have been published.

31. Thoreau's journals, March 27, 1841.

32. *The Annotated Walden,* edited by Philip Van Doren Stern (New York: Bramhall House, 1970), p. 70.

33. Richardson, p. 563.

34. The postmodern notion of *essentialism* as it relates to psychology is treated very differently. My use of the word comes from Aristotle and is used in a narrow context in relation to existence.

35. *The Essential Ernest Holmes* (New York: Tarcher/Penguin, 2002), p. 6.

36. Wallace Stevens, "Notes Toward a Supreme Fiction."

37. Just as the Ecology Hall of Fame begins on July 4, 1845, the day that Thoreau moved into his cabin, the latest entry is December 22, 1999, when Julia Butterfly Hill climbed down from Luna, the 180-foot California Coast redwood tree where she had lived for two years protecting it from loggers.

38. Loren Eiseley, *The Invisible Pyramid* (New York: Scribner's, 1970), p. 155.

39. Loren Eiseley, *The Mind As Nature* (New York: Harper & Row, 1962), p 42.

40. Eiseley, *The Mind As Nature,* pp. 60–61

41. Annie Dillard, *Three by Annie Dillard* (New York: Perennial, 1990), p. 260.

42. E. L. Doctorow, *Reporting the Universe* (Cambridge: Harvard University Press, 2003), p. 1.

SELECTED BIBLIOGRAPHY

Alcott, Amos Bronson. *The Journals of Bronson Alcott.* Edited by Odell Shepard. Boston: Little, Brown, 1938.

———. *How Like An Angel Came I Down.* Edited by Alice O. Howell. Hudson, N.Y.: Lindisfarne Press, 1991.

Cavell, Stanley. *Emerson's Transcendental Etudes.* Stanford, Calif.: Stanford University Press, 2003.

Dickinson, Emily. *The Collected Poems of Emily Dickinson.* New York: Barnes & Noble Books, 1993.

Dillard, Annie. *Three by Dillard.* New York: Perennial, 1990.

Doctorow, E. L. *Reporting the Universe.* Cambridge: Harvard University Press, 2003.

Eiseley, Loren. *The Mind as Nature.* New York: Harper & Row, 1962.

Emerson, Ralph Waldo. *The Collected Works of Ralph Waldo Emerson.* Edited by Alfred R. Ferguson, Joseph Slater, Douglas Emory Wilson, et al. 6 vols. to date. Cambridge: Harvard University Press, 1971–.

———. *The Journals and Miscellaneous Notebooks of Ralph Waldo Emerson.* Edited by William H. Gilman, Ralph H. Orth, et al. 16 vols. Cambridge: Harvard University Press, 1982.

Frothingham, Octavius B. *Transcendentalism in New England: A History.* New York, 1876; New York: Harper Torchbooks, 1959.

Fuller, Margaret. *The Writings of Margaret Fuller.* Edited by Mason Wade. New York, 1941.

Geldard, Richard. *The Spiritual Teachings of Ralph Waldo Emerson.* Hudson, N.Y.: Lindisfarne Press, 2001.

———. *God in Concord.* Burdett, N.Y.: Larson Publications, 1999.

Holmes, Ernest. *The Essential Ernest Holmes.* Edited by Rev. Jesse Jennings. New York: Tarcher/Penguin, 2002.

Miller, Perry. *The Transcendentalists: The Classic Anthology.* New York: MJF Books, 1978.

Myerson, Joel. *Transcendentalism: A Reader.* New York and London: Oxford University Press, 2000.

Reed, Sampson. *Observations on the Growth of the Mind.* Boston, 1826.

Richardson, Robert D., Jr. *Emerson: The Mind on Fire.* Berkeley: University of California Press, 1995.

Robinson, David, ed. *The Political Emerson.* Boston: Beacon Press, 2004.

Stevens, Wallace. *The Palm at the End of the Mind: Selected Poems.* New York: Vintage Books, 1972.

Thoreau, Henry David. *Walden and Other Writings of Henry David Thoreau.* New York: Modern Library, 1965.

———. *The Annotated Walden.* Edited by Philip Van Doren Stern. New York: Bramhall House, 1970.

———. *The Journals of Henry David Thoreau,* 16 vols. Salt Lake City: Peregrine Smith Books, 1984.

Whitman, Walt. *Whitman: Poetry and Prose.* New York: Library of America, 1982.

INDEX

ABOUT THE EDITOR

RICHARD G. GELDARD is a graduate of Bowdoin College, Bread Loaf School of English, and Stanford University, where he earned his doctorate. He has taught English and philosophy at the secondary, undergraduate, and graduate levels. Among his books are three devoted to Ralph Waldo Emerson and another to the pre-Socratic philosopher Heraclitus. He is a member of the board of directors of the Ralph Waldo Emerson Institute and senior adviser to RWE.org, a leading Emerson website.